the TREASURE PRINCIPLE

RANDY ALCORN

Learning Activities and Leader Guide
by Debbie Kubik Evert

LifeWay Press®
Nashville, Tennessee

ISBN 1-4158-2015-5

This book is the resource for course CG-1067 in the subject area Personal Life in the Christian Growth Study Plan.

Dewey Decimal classification: 177
Subject headings: GENEROSITY \ JOY AND SORROW

Photography: Graham Chalmers, PictureQuest
Inset: Michael Gomez

To order additional copies of this resource, WRITE to LifeWay Church Resources Customer Service; One LifeWay Plaza; Nashville, TN 37234-0113; FAX (615) 251-5933; PHONE toll free (800) 458-2772; E-MAIL *orderentry@lifeway.com;* ORDER ONLINE at *www.lifeway.com;* or VISIT the LifeWay Christian Store serving you.

Printed in the United States of America

Leadership and Adult Publishing
LifeWay Church Resources
One LifeWay Plaza
Nashville, TN 37234-0175

Contents

About the Author

Randy Alcorn, a former pastor and a bestselling author, is the founder and director of Eternal Perspective Ministries (EPM), a nonprofit organization dedicated to teaching biblical truth and drawing attention to the needy. EPM exists to meet the needs of the unreached, unfed, unborn, uneducated, unreconciled, and unsupported people around the world. "My ministry focus is communicating the strategic importance of using our earthly time, money, possessions, and opportunities to invest in need-meeting ministries that count for eternity," Alcorn says. "I do that by trying to analyze, teach, and apply the implications of Christian truth."

Alcorn's novels include *Deadline, Dominion, Edge of Eternity, Lord Foulgrin's Letters, The Ishbane Conspiracy,* and *Safely Home.* His nonfiction books include *The Purity Principle; The Grace and Truth Paradox; In Light of Eternity; ProLife Answers to ProChoice Arguments; Money, Possessions, and Eternity;* and *Heaven.*

Alcorn attended Multnomah Bible College and Western Seminary, where he received his bachelor of theology, master of arts in biblical studies, and doctor of divinity. He and his wife, Nanci, live in Gresham, Oregon, and have two married daughters, Karina Franklin and Angela Stump.

Preface

Jesus said a lot about money and possessions. This topic constituted 15 percent of all His teachings. Why? Because there's a connection between our spiritual lives and our money. The way we value and use money reveals the nature of our hearts. As Jesus said, " 'Where your treasure is, there your heart will be also' " (Matt. 6:21).

Jesus wants us to invest in treasures that will last. Warning us about the futility of collecting treasures on earth, He encourages us to discover the joy of collecting treasures in heaven. By investing in eternity while we are still on earth, we live the truth of the Treasure Principle: You can't take it with you, but you can send it on ahead.

This study uses Scripture to teach you how to use money and possessions to invest in heaven. You will discover what it means to collect heavenly treasures, and you will recognize the infinite value of heavenly treasures over earthly ones. You will acknowledge God's ownership of all things as you accept your role as His money manager. Six biblical keys will help you understand and live the Treasure Principle in your daily choices about using your resources. By understanding the importance of giving to God's kingdom, you will get a glimpse of the joy that comes to those who take every opportunity to invest in eternity.

The Treasure Principle is like hidden treasure that, once discovered, brings life-changing joy. When you possess its eternal riches, you'll never be content with less.

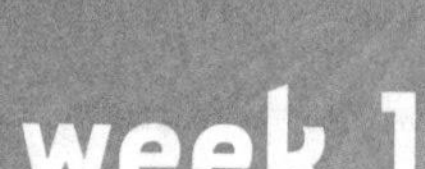

Investing in Eternity

day 1

Hidden Treasure

A first-century Hebrew walks alone on a hot afternoon, staff in hand. His shoulders are stooped, sandals covered with dirt, tunic stained with sweat. But he doesn't stop to rest. He has pressing business in the city.

He veers off the road into a field, seeking a shortcut. The owner won't mind. Travelers are permitted this courtesy. To keep his balance in the uneven field, the man thrusts his staff into the dirt. Thunk! The staff strikes something hard.

He stops, wipes his brow, and pokes again. Thunk! *Something's under there, and it's not a rock,* he says to himself.

The traveler can't afford to linger, but his curiosity won't let him go. He jabs at the ground. Something reflects a sliver of sunlight. He drops to his knees and starts digging.

Five minutes later he's uncovered it—a case fringed in gold. By the looks of it, the chest has been there for decades. Heart racing, he pries off the rusty lock and opens the lid.

Gold coins! Jewelry! Precious stones of every color! A treasure more valuable than anything he's ever imagined.

Hands shaking, the traveler inspects the coins, issued in Rome more than 70 years ago. Surely the current landowner has no clue that the treasure is here.

What do you think the traveler will do?

- ☐ Grab the chest and get out of there!
- ☐ Bury the chest, but mark the spot.
- ☐ Take the contents and bury an empty chest.
- ☐ Walk away and get no further involved.

The traveler closes the lid, buries the chest, and marks the spot. He turns around, heading home—only now he's skipping like a little boy, smiling broadly. As he races home, he thinks: *What an unbelievable find! I must have that treasure! But I can't just take it—that would be stealing. Whoever owns the field owns what's in it. But how can I afford to buy it? I'll sell my farm … and crops … all my tools … my prize oxen. If I sell everything, that should be enough.*

From the moment of his discovery, the traveler's life changes. The treasure captures his imagination and becomes the stuff of his dreams. It's his reference point, his new center of gravity. With every step he has this treasure in mind.

Jesus captured this story in a single verse.

Underline what Jesus compared the treasure to.

THE KINGDOM OF HEAVEN IS LIKE TREASURE, BURIED IN A FIELD, THAT A MAN FOUND AND REBURIED. THEN IN HIS JOY HE GOES AND SELLS EVERYTHING HE HAS AND BUYS THAT FIELD. *MATTHEW 13:44*

The parable of hidden treasure is one of many references Jesus made to the kingdom of heaven. It's also one of His many references to money and possessions. In fact, 15 percent of everything Christ said relates to this topic—more than all of His combined teachings on heaven and hell.

Why do you think Jesus taught so much about money and material possessions?

____

____

Jesus emphasized money and possessions because He saw a fundamental connection between our spiritual lives and how we think about and handle money. We may try to divorce our faith and our finances, but God sees them as inseparable.

Years ago I came to this realization while reading Luke 3. John the Baptist was preaching to crowds of people who had gathered to hear him and be baptized.

Stop and read Luke 3:1-15 in your Bible.

Three different groups asked John what they should do to bear the fruit of repentance. When John told them to " 'produce fruit consistent with repentance' " (v. 8), each group asked him a very similar question.

What question did the crowds ask?

____

John's response is found in verse 11: " 'The one who has two shirts must share with someone who has none, and the one who has food must do the same.' " This probably wasn't the answer they expected. They probably felt confused and frustrated.

A second group asked John the same question.

Who was this group? ______________________

Write the word added to its question: ______________

This group recognized John as a teacher. He answered, " 'Don't collect any more than what you have been authorized' " (v. 13). Do you think they were satisfied with his answer?

What did they do?

- ❑ Scripture doesn't say.
- ❑ They left grumbling.

A third group, soldiers, asked John the same question.

How did John answer them in verse 14?

____

____

Each group had asked what it should do to demonstrate the fruit of spiritual transformation " 'consistent with repentance' " (v. 8). Yet each of John's answers related to money and possessions. With remarkable spiritual discernment John pinpointed the specific need that was keeping each group from truly repenting and turning to God.

Draw lines between the columns to connect John's answer to each group's need.

Crowds	" 'Don't take money from anyone by force or false accusation; be satisfied with your wages.' "
Tax collectors	" 'The one who has two shirts must share with someone who has none, and the one who has food must do the same.' "
Soldiers	" 'Don't collect any more than what you have been authorized.' "

No wonder some in the crowd thought John was the Messiah. He spoke directly to their hearts!

After reading these verses, I realized that our approach to money and possessions isn't just important. It's central to our spiritual lives. It's of such high priority to God that John the Baptist couldn't talk about spirituality without talking about how to handle money and possessions.

The connection between money and our spiritual lives is equally important for believers today. Gaining the kingdom of God is like discovering hidden treasure. Over the next four weeks you'll study Scriptures that teach you how to use money and possessions to invest in God's kingdom. You'll discover the infinite value of heavenly treasures over earthly ones and biblical keys for collecting treasures in heaven. And you'll get a glimpse of the joy that comes from investing in God's kingdom. The biblical principles I will share changed my life. I pray that they will do the same for you.

THE DAY IN REVIEW

Review today's lesson.
What was the most important concept you read today?

____

____

How will this truth challenge you to be like Christ?

____

____

Pray, asking God to use this study to help you value His kingdom as a priceless treasure and learn ways to invest in His kingdom. Write your prayer below.

____

____

____

____

____

____

____

Money Matters

day 2

In day 1 we observed that a connection exists between God and money. Today we'll meet several people who discovered that connection.

Read Luke 19:1-10 in your Bible.

Zacchaeus was so anxious to see Jesus that he climbed a tree to get a better look.

What was Jesus' reaction to Zacchaeus?

- ❑ "Hey, Buddy, get out of that tree! You'll fall!"
- ❑ "Hurry and come down! I'm staying at your house today."
- ❑ Jesus walked by without acknowledging him.

Can you imagine Zacchaeus's excitement? Jesus was going to his house! The people must have thought Jesus was crazy to visit the home of a sinner. Crazy or not, Jesus would soon be at his house. Without hesitation Zacchaeus scooted down the tree and stood before Jesus. He said to Jesus: " 'Look, I'll give half of my possessions to the poor, Lord! And if I have extorted anything from anyone, I'll pay back four times as much!' " (v. 8).

Did you miss something? Where was Jesus' sermon to His new friend about his sinful behavior? Didn't Jesus scold this tax collector for taking more than his share of the people's taxes? No! Standing before Jesus, this government worker was transformed.

How did Jesus respond to Zacchaeus's words?

____

Salvation! Zacchaeus's radical new approach to money proved that his heart had been transformed.

Next we meet a group of Jerusalem converts who eagerly sold their possessions to give to the needy.

Read Acts 2:44-45; 4:32-35 in your Bible. How did the believers demonstrate an understanding of the proper relationship between God and money or possessions?

❑ Distributed wealth to the needy
❑ Sold possessions and property
❑ Gave their money to the Pharisees

These believers not only understood the connection between their spiritual and financial lives but also put it into practice.

A poor widow steps off the pages of Scripture by giving.

Read Mark 12:41-44 in your Bible.

Did the rich people give a lot of money?	❑ Yes	❑ No
Did they give everything they had?	❑ Yes	❑ No
Did this woman give a lot of money?	❑ Yes	❑ No
Did she give everything she had?	❑ Yes	❑ No

Which action did Jesus commend? ________________

In contrast to the poor widow, a rich young man approached Jesus as He was setting off on a journey.

Read Mark 10:17-22 in your Bible.
What question did the young man ask Jesus?

____

Perhaps the man thought he could purchase something or do a good work to earn his way into God's kingdom. However, Jesus recognized that the man knew the law and stated several commandments that should be kept. *So far, so good,* the young man must have thought. He had kept all of the commandments.

Then Jesus lovingly looked this man in the face and told him he lacked something. Keep in mind that this man probably had everything he had ever wanted. Yet he lacked one thing.

What did Jesus tell him?

- ❑ "Give more money to the church."
- ❑ "Go and preach the good news."
- ❑ "Go, sell all you have and give to the poor, and you will have treasure in heaven. Then come, follow Me."

Ouch! Jesus hit a very tender spot while striking the very core of the connection between His Father and money.

How did the young man react?

____

The young man "was stunned at this demand, and he went away grieving, because he had many possessions" (v. 22).

The man was obsessed with earthly treasures, but Jesus called him to something higher—heavenly treasures. Jesus knew that money and possessions were the man's god. He realized that the man wouldn't serve God unless he dethroned his money idol. But the seeker considered the price too great. Sadly, he walked away from real treasures.

The rich young man wasn't willing to give up everything for a greater treasure, but our traveler in the field was. Why? Because he understood what he would gain. Do you feel sorry for the traveler? After all, his discovery cost him everything. We shouldn't pity this man. We should envy him! His sacrifice pales in comparison to his reward. Consider the costs-to-benefits ratio. The benefits far outweigh the costs.

Write the costs and benefits of the traveler's decision to get the treasure. I've supplied one for you.

Costs	Benefits
Everything he owned	Everything that mattered

The traveler made short-term sacrifices to obtain a long-term reward. Matthew 13:44 says that " 'in his joy' " the traveler sold his possessions and bought the field. He wasn't exchanging lesser treasures for greater treasures from dutiful drudgery but from joyful exhilaration. He would have been a fool not to do exactly what he did.

Check the character(s) you most closely resemble in your attitudes and actions.

- ❑ Like Zacchaeus, willing to make things right by repaying
- ❑ Like the believers in Acts, willing to give to the needy
- ❑ Like the widow, willing to give all
- ❑ Like the rich young man, unwilling to give up wealth to follow Christ
- ❑ Like the traveler, willing to sacrifice earthly possessions to gain eternal reward

THE DAY IN REVIEW

Review today's lesson.
What was the most important concept you read today?

___

How will this truth challenge you to be like Christ?

___

___

Pray about your response to the final activity in today's lesson. Ask God to make you more willing to give all to follow Him and to invest in His kingdom. Write your prayer below.

___

___

___

___

___

Treasures on Earth

day 3

Jesus' story about treasure in the field is an object lesson about heavenly treasure. Of course, no matter how great the value of that earthly fortune, it will be worthless in eternity. In fact, it's exactly this kind of treasure that people waste their lives pursuing. Jesus appealed to what we value—temporary, earthly treasure—to make an analogy about what we should value—eternal, heavenly treasure.

In Matthew 6 Jesus unveiled His foundational teaching on earthly and heavenly treasures.

DON'T COLLECT FOR YOURSELVES TREASURES ON EARTH, WHERE MOTH AND RUST DESTROY AND WHERE THIEVES BREAK IN AND STEAL. BUT COLLECT FOR YOURSELVES TREASURES IN HEAVEN, WHERE NEITHER MOTH NOR RUST DESTROYS, AND WHERE THIEVES DON'T BREAK IN AND STEAL. FOR WHERE YOUR TREASURE IS, THERE YOUR HEART WILL BE ALSO. *MATTHEW 6:19-21*

Why did Jesus tell us not to collect treasures on earth?

- ☐ Earthly treasures are bad.
- ☐ Earthly treasures do not last.

Jesus taught that storing treasures on earth is futile because they do not last. I really like Solomon's analogy in Proverbs 23:4-5:

DON'T WEAR YOURSELF OUT TO GET RICH;
STOP GIVING YOUR ATTENTION TO IT.
AS SOON AS YOUR EYES FLY TO IT, IT DISAPPEARS,
FOR IT MAKES WINGS FOR ITSELF
AND FLIES LIKE AN EAGLE TO THE SKY.

Think about your most prized possession. Now imagine it sprouting wings and flying off. Sooner or later it will disappear.

Read more verses Solomon wrote in Proverbs and Ecclesiastes. Match the verses with their references.

___ 1. Proverbs 11:28
___ 2. Proverbs 27:24
___ 3. Proverbs 28:22
___ 4. Ecclesiastes 5:10

a. "A greedy man is in a hurry for wealth; he doesn't know that poverty will come to him."
b. "Anyone trusting in riches will fall, but the righteous will flourish like foliage."
c. "The one who loves money is never satisfied with money, and whoever loves wealth is never satisfied with income."
d. "Wealth is not forever; not even a crown lasts for all time."

Solomon knew what he was talking about. He had a chance to ask God for riches and all kinds of earthly treasures. Instead, he asked for something else.

Read 2 Chronicles 1:7-12 in your Bible.

What did Solomon ask for? ______________________________

What else did God grant Solomon? ________________________

Solomon got the riches he didn't ask for, but he asked for wisdom first. What he received was " 'not like this for the kings who were before you, nor will it be like this for those after you' " (v. 12).

When Jesus warned us not to collect treasures on earth, it's not just because wealth *might* be lost; it's because wealth will *always* be lost. Either it leaves us while we live, or we leave it when we die. No exceptions! According to Jesus, storing up earthly treasures isn't simply wrong. It's just plain stupid!

Look at something else Jesus taught about earthly riches.

I ASSURE YOU: IT WILL BE HARD FOR A RICH PERSON TO ENTER THE KINGDOM OF HEAVEN! AGAIN I TELL YOU, IT IS EASIER FOR A CAMEL TO GO THROUGH THE EYE OF A NEEDLE THAN FOR A RICH PERSON TO ENTER THE KINGDOM OF HEAVEN. *MATTHEW 19:23-24*

Which statement accurately summarizes what Jesus said?

- ❑ A wealthy person who puts riches before God cannot enter the kingdom.
- ❑ A wealthy person isn't welcome in God's kingdom.

If a wealthy person puts his riches before his relationship with God, his priorities are misplaced. Like the rich young man, the wealthy person walks away from God grieved.

Jesus made still another statement about wealth on earth.

NO ONE CAN BE A SLAVE OF TWO MASTERS, SINCE EITHER HE WILL HATE ONE AND LOVE THE OTHER, OR BE DEVOTED TO ONE AND DESPISE THE OTHER. YOU CANNOT BE SLAVES OF GOD AND OF MONEY. *MATTHEW 6:24*

You cannot be a slave of both God and money. The dual allegiance won't work.

Are you a slave ❑ to God or ❑ to money?

Give evidence for your answer.

____

____

____

Paul also warned us not to place too much emphasis on earthly treasures:

THOSE WHO WANT TO BE RICH FALL INTO TEMPTATION, A TRAP, AND MANY FOOLISH AND HARMFUL DESIRES, WHICH PLUNGE PEOPLE INTO RUIN AND DESTRUCTION. FOR THE LOVE OF MONEY IS A ROOT OF ALL KINDS OF EVIL, AND BY CRAVING IT, SOME HAVE WANDERED AWAY FROM THE FAITH AND PIERCED THEMSELVES WITH MANY PAINS. *1 TIMOTHY 6:9–10*

What is waiting for people who want to get rich?

- ❑ Temptation
- ❑ A trap
- ❑ Blessings
- ❑ Foolish and harmful desires
- ❑ A long life
- ❑ Eternal rewards

What is the result of foolish and harmful desires?

____

Is money evil? ❑ Yes ❑ No

What is the result of craving money?

____

____

Those who want to get rich will fall into temptation that can plunge them into ruin and destruction. Money is not evil, but loving it is the root of all kinds of evil. Paul said that some who crave money have "wandered away from the faith and pierced themselves with many pains" (v. 10). Money—and wanting more of it—became far more important than serving God and having faith that He will provide what is needed.

Paul also wrote:

GODLINESS WITH CONTENTMENT IS A GREAT GAIN.
FOR WE BROUGHT NOTHING INTO THE WORLD,
AND WE CAN TAKE NOTHING OUT. *1 TIMOTHY 6:6–7*

Have you ever seen a U-Haul behind a hearse?

Assess the way you view money by marking the continuum.

I love money and want more.	I know wealth doesn't last, but I enjoy its benefits.	I am content with God's provision.

THE DAY IN REVIEW

Review today's lesson.
What was the most important concept you read today?

____

____

How will this truth challenge you to be like Christ?

____

____

Pray about your response to the final activity in today's lesson. Ask God to help you recognize the transience of riches and to be content with what you have in Him. Write your prayer below.

____

____

____

____

____

____

____

____

____

____

____

Treasures in Heaven

day 4

Jesus didn't just tell us where not to put our treasures. After warning us about the futility of collecting treasures on earth, He also gave the best investment advice we'll ever hear.

Underline the place Jesus advised us to make investments.

COLLECT FOR YOURSELVES TREASURES IN HEAVEN, WHERE NEITHER MOTH NOR RUST DESTROYS, AND WHERE THIEVES DON'T BREAK IN AND STEAL.
MATTHEW 6:20

What are treasures in heaven? They include pleasure, possessions, and power. God has created each of us with desires for these three things. At first this idea may sound unbiblical, because we typically think of these things as temptations. True, Satan tempts us in each of these areas. If we give in, the desire for pleasure can degenerate into hedonism, the desire for possessions into materialism, and the desire for power into egotism.

Use a dictionary to define these terms.

Hedonism: ______________________________

____

Materialism: ______________________________

____

Egotism: ______________________________

____

These extremes result when we let Satan fulfill our desires for pleasure, possessions, and power. Satan tempted Jesus in the same three areas.

Read Luke 4:1-13 in your Bible and identify Satan's three temptations and Jesus' three responses.

Satan's Temptations	**Jesus' Responses**
____________	____________
____________	____________
____________	____________

Go back and place a check mark beside the appeal to pleasure, an *X* beside the appeal to possessions, and a star beside the appeal to power.

Satan tempted God's Son to make bread for the pleasure of eating, to worship him for the possession of all the world's kingdoms, and to cast Himself from the temple for the power of commanding angelic intervention. Instead of giving in, Jesus answered each temptation with Scripture. We are wise to follow His example.

I can see the words forming on your lips right now: "You said the desires for pleasure, possessions, and power are treasures in heaven. If they make us vulnerable to temptation, how can they be good?" Satan can appeal to the desires for these things only because our Creator built those desires into us. From the very beginning, God designed us to want these things. And Satan knew just how to appeal to those desires.

Read Genesis 3:1-7 in your Bible. Had Adam and Eve already sinned when the serpent tempted them? ❑ Yes ❑ No

The draw to pleasure, possessions, and power cannot be rooted in our sin nature, because Satan appealed to these desires in Adam and Eve before they were sinful. Similarly, Christ had no sin nature. Satan knew this. Yet he appealed to Him on the same three grounds. Why? Because Christ was human, and to be human is to want these things. We want pleasure, possessions, and power not because we are sinful but because we are human.

If this argument seems unconvincing, consider the clincher: God Himself appeals to each of these desires in us! He offers us pleasure, possessions, and power in His eternal kingdom.

Read Matthew 6:1-18 in your Bible. Draw lines across the columns to match the disciplines with their definitions.

Giving	Denying personal power to gain power from God
Prayer	Denying the possession of riches to gain possessions from God
Fasting	Denying the pleasure of eating to gain pleasure in God

Eating, owning, and ruling are not bad, but in giving, prayer, and fasting we temporarily abstain from them to accomplish a higher kingdom purpose.

Our sin nature has tainted pleasure, possessions, and power in this world. But in eternity we'll be able to handle these things because we'll be without sin. As our sinless Lord handles them properly, we will be able to handle them properly.

Fulfilling desires and seeking rewards are not unchristian. What is unchristian is a self-centeredness that is unconcerned about God and neighbor. Also unchristian is a preoccupation with the immediate fulfilling of desires that distracts us from finding our ultimate fulfillment in Christ.

Check the statement that most accurately describes you.

- ❑ I am pursuing pleasure, possessions, and power by accumulating wealth for myself and by seeking self-gratification.
- ❑ I am pursuing pleasure, possessions, and power by giving to others and by seeking God's will for using my resources.

Someone who gives his life, money, and possessions to receive rewards from God—the greatest of which is the resounding statement "Well done"—is someone whose deepest thirsts will be eternally quenched by the Maker and Fulfiller of desire.

In Portland, Oregon, is a row of big, beautiful new houses called the Street of Dreams. While the houses are fun to look at, I'm struck with the thought of how sad it would be to have a dream as small as one of those houses.

When I was a pastor, a couple told me they wanted to give more money to the church and to missions. "But we've always had this dream for a beautiful home in the country," they added, "and we can't seem to shake it. Is that wrong?"

I told them I thought the dream of a perfect place comes from God, but the dream will not be fulfilled in this life. Our dream house is coming; we don't have to build it here. In fact, we can't. Any dream house on earth will eventually be ravaged by time, floods, earthquakes, tornadoes, carpenter ants, freeways—you name it. And who would want to divert kingdom funds to a dream house on earth if you know that it will burn to the ground, with no insurance company left to cover the loss? Instead, why not send building materials ahead to the Carpenter, who is building your dream house in heaven?

THE DAY IN REVIEW

Review today's lesson.
What was the most important concept you read today?

____

How will this truth challenge you to be like Christ?

____

Ask God to help you focus on treasures in heaven as you follow His plan for gaining pleasure, possessions, and power. Write your prayer below.

____

____

____

____

The Ultimate Treasure

day 5

Are your earthly possessions worthless? It's not a trick question. However, you can't answer it without making a comparison—without placing your earthly treasures against your heavenly treasures.

Read Philippians 3:7-11 in your Bible.

Now let me rephrase the question.

Compared to Jesus and heavenly treasures, are your earthly possessions worthless? ❑ Yes ❑ No

Verse 8 says that the things we have on earth are filth.

In verses 7-8 underline words that express Paul's losses. Circle what he said he gained.

EVERYTHING THAT WAS A GAIN TO ME, I HAVE CONSIDERED TO BE A LOSS BECAUSE OF CHRIST. MORE THAN THAT, I ALSO CONSIDER EVERYTHING TO BE A LOSS IN VIEW OF THE SURPASSING VALUE OF KNOWING CHRIST JESUS MY LORD. BECAUSE OF HIM I HAVE SUFFERED THE LOSS OF ALL THINGS AND CONSIDER THEM FILTH, SO THAT I MAY GAIN CHRIST.

Why did Paul describe everything as a loss and filth? Because of Christ. Christ Himself is our ultimate treasure. All else pales in comparison to Him and the joy of knowing Him.

Three kinds of treasures will last. A person, Jesus, is our first treasure. A place, heaven, is our second treasure. Possessions, eternal rewards, are our third treasure.

Mark one choice under each statement to indicate your belief about each treasure.

Jesus is my treasure.

- ❑ I've never thought of Jesus as my treasure.
- ❑ Jesus is one of my treasures, but I struggle with having joy in Him completely.
- ❑ Jesus is absolutely my treasure.

Heaven is my treasure.

- ❑ I haven't thought of heaven as a treasure.
- ❑ Heaven is a place I want to go, but I don't think of it as a treasure. I like it here too.
- ❑ I can't wait to get to heaven, the place I treasure.

Eternal rewards are my treasure.

- ❑ Earthly possessions are everything to me. Having them makes me feel good.
- ❑ I like my earthly possessions, but I have begun to collect treasures in heaven.
- ❑ My treasures are mostly in heaven, not on earth.

" 'Collect for yourselves treasures in heaven' " (Matt. 6:20). Why? Because it's right? Not just that but also because it's smart. Such treasures will last. Jesus argued from the bottom line. It's not an emotional appeal; it's a logical one: invest in what has lasting value.

This isn't a new concept. We also find it in the Psalms.

Read Psalm 49:16-20 in your Bible. What will a wealthy man take with him when he dies?

____

Does this fact change if the person was well respected or held an important position? ❑ Yes ❑ No

John D. Rockefeller was one of the wealthiest men who ever lived. After he died, someone asked his accountant, "How much money did John D. leave?" The reply was classic: "He left all of it."

You can't take it with you. Jesus took that profound truth and added a stunning qualification. By telling us to collect treasures for ourselves in heaven, He gave us a breathtaking corollary, which I call the Treasure Principle:

You can't take it with you, but you can send it on ahead.

It's that simple. If it doesn't take your breath away, you don't understand its profound meaning!

Write in your own words what you think the Treasure Principle means.

____

____

Anything we try to hang on to here will be lost, but anything we put into God's hands will be ours for eternity. And it's insured by the real FDIC, the Father's Deposit Insurance Corporation. If we give instead of keep, if we invest in the eternal instead of in the temporal, we collect treasures in heaven that never stop paying dividends. The treasures we collect on earth will be left behind when we leave. The treasures we collect in heaven will be waiting for us when we arrive.

Suppose I offer you $1,000 today to spend any way you want. Not a bad deal. But suppose I give you a choice: you can either have that $1,000 today or $10 million one year from now, then $10 million more every year after that. Only a fool would take $1,000 today. Yet that's what we do when we grab something that will last for only a moment, forgoing something far more valuable that we could enjoy later and for much longer. The money God entrusts to us here on earth is eternal investment capital. Every day is an opportunity to buy more shares in His kingdom.

Write the Treasure Principle.

___

I guarantee that if you embrace this revolutionary concept, it will change your life. As you collect heavenly treasures, you'll gain an everlasting version of what the first-century Hebrew found in the hidden treasure. Joy.

Reread Matthew 13:44 and circle the word *joy*.

THE KINGDOM OF HEAVEN IS LIKE TREASURE, BURIED IN A FIELD, THAT A MAN FOUND AND REBURIED. THEN IN HIS JOY HE GOES AND SELLS EVERYTHING HE HAS AND BUYS THAT FIELD. *MATTHEW 13:44*

Let that verse remind you of what lies ahead.

THE DAY IN REVIEW

Review today's lesson.
What was the most important concept you read today?

___

How will this truth challenge you to be like Christ?

___

Praise Jesus as the ultimate treasure. Ask God to fill you with joy as you discover ways to collect heavenly treasures. Write your prayer below.

___

___

___

___

___

God Is the Owner

day 1

Yours or God's?

In 1990 I was a pastor of a large church, making a good salary and earning book royalties. I had been a pastor for 13 years, and I didn't want to do anything else.

Then something happened that turned our lives upside down. I was on the board of a crisis-pregnancy center, and we had opened our home to a pregnant teenager, helping her give up her baby for adoption. We also had the joy of seeing her come to Christ.

After this experience I felt an even greater burden for the unborn. After searching Scripture and praying a lot, I began participating in peaceful, nonviolent rescues at abortion clinics. For this I was arrested and sent to jail. An abortion clinic won a court judgment against a group of us. I told a judge that I would pay anything I owed, but I couldn't give money to people who would use it to kill babies.

Then I discovered that my church would receive a writ of garnishment demanding that it surrender one-fourth of my wages each month to the abortion clinic. The church would either have to pay the abortion clinic or defy a court order. To prevent this from happening, I resigned.

I had already divested myself of book royalties. The only way I could avoid garnishment was to make no more than minimum wage. Fortunately, our family had been living on only a portion of my church salary, and we had just made our final house payment, so we were out of debt.

Another court judgment followed, involving another abortion clinic. Though our actions had been nonviolent, the clinic was awarded the largest judgment ever against a group of peaceful protesters: $8.4 million. This time it seemed likely that we would lose our house.

By all appearances and certainly by the world's standards, our lives had taken a devastating turn. Right? We chose to look at the situation from God's point of view:

YOU PLANNED EVIL AGAINST ME; GOD PLANNED IT FOR GOOD TO BRING ABOUT THE PRESENT RESULT. *GENESIS 50:20*

So what did we do? We began a new ministry. My wife, Nanci, worked at a secretary's salary, supplementing my minimum wage. Her name alone was on all our assets, including the house. My inability to own assets legally was nothing I sought and nothing to earn congratulations, but God used it to help me understand what He means by " 'Everything under heaven belongs to Me' " (Job 41:11). Job learned this lesson long before I did.

Read Job 1:1-3 in your Bible.
Check the phrases that describe Job.

- ❑ Perfect integrity
- ❑ Turned away from evil
- ❑ An immoral man
- ❑ An idolater
- ❑ Feared God

Who were Job's family members? ______________________

What did Job own? ______________________________

____

Satan approached God and asked whether he could test this "man of perfect integrity" (v. 1). God allowed him to do so.

Read Job 1:6-22. What happened to Job's possessions?

- ❑ Multiplied
- ❑ Swept up by a storm
- ❑ Stolen
- ❑ Raided
- ❑ Servants killed

What happened to Job's children?

- ❑ Nothing
- ❑ Crushed by a house during a party
- ❑ Struck down by a plague

Job lost his oxen and donkeys to the Sabeans and his camels to the Chaldeans. These groups also slaughtered Job's servants. A lightning storm killed his sheep. His seven sons and three daughters were at the older brother's house when a storm leveled the house they were in. They all died.

How did Job respond to these disasters?

Tore his ______________

Shaved his________________

Fell to the ________________ and ______________________

Did Job blame God for what happened? ❑ Yes ❑ No

Verse 22 sums it up: "Throughout all this Job did not sin or blame God for anything." Wow!

A second test came to Job in chapter 2. Satan again asked God if he could test Job.

Read Job 2:4-8. What stipulation did God set this time?

____

What happened to Job? ________________________________

____

Although God stipulated that Satan spare Job's life, God allowed him to harm Job's health this time. Consequently, Job was infected with boils all over his body.

The only family member Job had left was his wife. Observe the way she responded to Job's calamity:

DO YOU STILL RETAIN YOUR INTEGRITY? CURSE GOD AND DIE! *JOB 2:9*

Hmm. Not very supportive. But Job's answer is one to emulate:

SHOULD WE ACCEPT ONLY GOOD FROM GOD AND NOT ADVERSITY? THROUGHOUT ALL THIS JOB DID NOT SIN IN WHAT HE SAID. *JOB 2:10*

Job was willing to accept not only good from God but also adversity.

Having my wages garnisheed wasn't the first time God had taught me about His ownership. Many years ago I had loaned a new portable stereo to our church's high-school group. It came back beat-up, and I admit that it bothered me. But the Lord convicted me, reminding me that it wasn't my stereo. It was His. And it had been used to help reach young people. Who was I to complain about what was God's?

Back then the material possessions I valued most were my books. My money went toward purchasing thousands of them, and those books meant a lot to me. I lent them to people, but I was troubled when they weren't returned or came back in worn condition.

Then I sensed God's leading to hand over the books—all of them—to begin a church library. I looked at the names of those who checked them out, sometimes dozens of names for each book. I realized that by releasing the books, I had invested in others' lives. Suddenly, the more worn the book, the better. My perspective totally changed.

Just as Job didn't consider his life his own, I learned that what I think I own, I really don't. My books, my house, my money—everything belongs to God. This wasn't an easy lesson to learn, but when I did, it gave me the right perspective on money and possessions.

Name the material object you value most. ______________

Have you ever thought that God owns that object?

❑ Yes ❑ No

How will that realization change the way you use the object?

____

____

THE DAY IN REVIEW

Review today's lesson.

What was the most important concept you read today?

____

How will this truth challenge you to be like Christ?

____

____

Pray, using Job's words in Job 1:21 to acknowledge God's ownership of everything you have. Write your prayer below.

____

____

____

____

____

____

Managing God's Accounts

day 2

God used the court judgments you read about yesterday to take my understanding of His ownership to a new level. The following Scripture passages really hit home.

Read the verses and answer the questions that follow.

You may say to yourself, "My power and my own ability have gained this wealth for me," but remember that the Lord your God gives you the power to gain wealth, in order to confirm His covenant He swore to your fathers, as it is today. If you ever forget the Lord your God and go after other gods to worship and bow down to them, I testify against you today that you will perish. *Deuteronomy 8:17-19*

What is the source of the power to gain wealth?

- ❑ It comes naturally.
- ❑ I work to get it.
- ❑ God gives me the power.

The earth and everything in it,
the world and its inhabitants,
belong to the Lord;
for He laid its foundation on the seas
and established it on the rivers. *Psalm 24:1-2*

"The silver and gold belong to Me"—the declaration of the Lord of Hosts. *Haggai 2:8*

Who owns the earth and everything in it? ________

Who owns the silver and gold? ____________

DO YOU NOT KNOW THAT YOUR BODY IS A SANCTUARY OF THE HOLY SPIRIT WHO IS IN YOU, WHOM YOU HAVE FROM GOD? YOU ARE NOT YOUR OWN, FOR YOU WERE BOUGHT AT A PRICE; THEREFORE GLORIFY GOD IN YOUR BODY.
1 CORINTHIANS 6:19-20

How is your body described?

____

Does your body belong to you? ❑ Yes ❑ No

Who owns it? ______________________________

Through various situations and Scripture passages like those you examined, God taught me the first of six keys to the Treasure Principle:

God owns everything. I'm His money manager.

God is the owner of everything, including books and stereos. He even owns me.

Ironically, I had written extensively about God's ownership in my book *Money, Possessions, and Eternity.* Within a year of its publication, I no longer owned anything, including that book. God was teaching me, in the crucible of adversity, the life-changing implications of that truth.

I realized that our house belonged to God, not us. Why worry about whether we would keep it if it belonged to Him anyway? He has no shortage of resources. He could easily provide us another place to live.

But understanding ownership was only half my lesson. If God was the owner, I was the manager. I needed to adopt a steward's mentality toward the assets He had entrusted to me. A steward manages assets for the owner's benefit. A steward carries no sense of entitlement for the assets he manages. His job is to find out what the owner wants done with his assets, then carry out his will.

Paul addressed stewardship several times in his letters.

Read 1 Corinthians 4:1-2. How did Paul describe himself?

- ❑ A servant of Christ
- ❑ A preacher
- ❑ An average guy
- ❑ A manager of God's mysteries

What is the responsibility of a manager?

____

A red flag should rise whenever we begin to think like owners. We should think like stewards and investment managers, always looking for the best place to invest the Owner's money. At the end of our term of service, we'll undergo a job-performance evaluation:

WE WILL ALL STAND BEFORE THE JUDGMENT SEAT OF GOD. SO THEN, EACH OF US WILL GIVE AN ACCOUNT OF HIMSELF TO GOD. *ROMANS 14:10,12*

Our name is on God's account, and we have unrestricted access to it. God trusts us, as His money managers, to set our own salaries. We draw needed funds from His wealth to pay our living expenses. One of our central spiritual decisions is determining what is a reasonable amount to live on. Whatever that amount is—and it will legitimately vary from person to person—we shouldn't hoard or spend the excess. After all, it's His, not ours. And He has something to say about where to put it.

Read Matthew 25:14-30 and record what each slave did.

The slave with five talents: ______________________

The slave with two talents: ______________________

The slave with one talent: ______________________

A talent was worth a large sum of money—about six thousand denarii. A denarius was equal to a day's wage for a common laborer. So a talent was the amount of money a slave would earn working six thousand days, or more than 16 years!

After being gone for a long time, the master returned home and found that the slave with five talents had earned five more for him. The one with two had earned two more. Notice the master's joyful response:

WELL DONE, GOOD AND FAITHFUL SLAVE! YOU WERE FAITHFUL OVER A FEW THINGS; I WILL PUT YOU IN CHARGE OF MANY THINGS. SHARE YOUR MASTER'S JOY! *MATTHEW 25:21,23*

And the slave with the one talent? His one talent was removed, and he was sent " 'into the outer darkness' " (v. 30). Instead of being called " 'good and faithful,' " his master called him a " 'good-for-nothing slave' " (vv. 21,23,30).

What is the lesson for those who don't have much?

____

____

If you make a small salary, don't minimize the amount entrusted to you and the importance of the way you handle it. The question isn't what you would do with a million dollars but what you will do with what God has already entrusted to you. What you do with what you earn now shows what you would do if you had more. That's why those who don't give when they make small incomes usually don't give when they make large ones.

Are you being faithful in managing what God has given you?

❑ Yes ❑ No

How does an understanding that you are God's money manager change the way you view your assets?

The only way to fireproof money and possessions is to give them back to God. That's the way to experience the greatest freedom and joy.

Write the Treasure Principle.

Write the first key to the Treasure Principle.

THE DAY IN REVIEW

Review today's lesson.
What was the most important concept you read today?

How will this truth challenge you to be like Christ?

Commit to God the resources He has entrusted to you.
Ask Him to help you be a good and faithful manager.
Write your prayer below.

The Privilege of Giving

day 3

Every spring Nanci and I read dozens of letters from people in our church who will go on summer missions trips and would like for us to pray and contribute financially. When this time comes each year, I'm like a kid in a candy store—a candy store as big as the world, as big as the heart of God.

Why are we so excited? Because we gain vested interest in God's work around the world, and we get to have a part in it. We see the enthusiasm, the growth, the kingdom-mindedness, and the changed priorities. We pray that those who go—as well as those who receive them—will never be the same. Recently I attended a gathering of givers. An older couple shared that they are traveling around the world getting involved in the ministries they support financially. Meanwhile, their home in the States is becoming rundown. They said: "Our children keep telling us: 'Fix up your house or buy a new one. You can afford it.' We tell them: 'Why would we do that? That's not what excites us!' "

That kind of excitement was evident among the Hebrews who were building the tabernacle in the Old Testament.

Read Exodus 36:4-7 in your Bible. What was the problem?

____

What did Moses do?

____

The people were so caught up in the excitement of giving that they had to be restrained. That's what giving will do to you.

Near the end of his life, David saw the people give their resources to build the temple.

Read 1 Chronicles 29:10-16.
What was the source of their giving?

____

These people understood that everything they had belonged to God. He was the source of the riches they gave back to Him.

Similarly, in the New Testament the Macedonian Christians understood the joy of giving:

WE WANT YOU TO KNOW, BROTHERS, ABOUT THE GRACE OF GOD GRANTED TO THE CHURCHES OF MACEDONIA: DURING A SEVERE TESTING BY AFFLICTION, THEIR ABUNDANCE OF JOY AND THEIR DEEP POVERTY OVERFLOWED INTO THE WEALTH OF THEIR GENEROSITY. I TESTIFY THAT, ON THEIR OWN, ACCORDING TO THEIR ABILITY AND BEYOND THEIR ABILITY, THEY BEGGED US INSISTENTLY FOR THE PRIVILEGE OF SHARING IN THE MINISTRY TO THE SAINTS, AND NOT JUST AS WE HAD HOPED. INSTEAD, THEY GAVE THEMSELVES ESPECIALLY TO THE LORD, THEN TO US BY GOD'S WILL. *2 CORINTHIANS 8:1-5*

Fill in the blanks.

In a time of severe testing by affliction, their abundance of _______ and their deep _______________ overflowed into the _____________ of their __________________.

Check the statement that is true.

- ❑ Paul had to beg the Macedonians to give.
- ❑ The Macedonians begged for the privilege of giving.

The Macedonians refused to let difficult circumstances keep them from joy. They had to plead for the opportunity to give this generously, presumably because Paul and others told them that their poverty exempted them from giving. These early Christians, though dirt poor, came up with every reason they could to give. They begged for the privilege of giving!

The people recognized an important fact: giving is an act of worship. Giving jump-starts our relationship with God. It opens our hands so that we can receive what God has for us. When we see what giving does for others and for us, we open our hands sooner and wider when the next opportunity comes.

In Isaiah 58:6-10 God said that His willingness to answer our prayers is directly affected by whether we care for the hungry, needy, and oppressed. Want to empower your prayer life? Give.

Read Isaiah 58:6-10 in your Bible and list examples of giving in these verses.

____

____

____

____

Check some benefits of giving, according to this passage.

- ❑ You'll get a great tax write-off.
- ❑ Your light will shine in the darkness.
- ❑ Your recovery will come quickly.
- ❑ God will reward you with earthly possessions.
- ❑ Your righteousness will go before you.
- ❑ The Lord's glory will be your rear guard.
- ❑ God will answer you when you call.
- ❑ A ministry will honor you at a banquet for major donors.

Caring for the needy flows from knowing God, and it draws us closer to Him. This cycle brings us perpetual blessing.

Giving also brings freedom. It's a matter of basic physics. The greater the mass, the greater the hold that mass exerts. The more things we own—the greater their total mass—the more they grip us, setting us in orbit around them. Finally, like a black hole, they suck us in. Giving changes all that. It breaks us out of orbit around our possessions. We escape their gravity, allowing us to enter a new orbit around our treasures in heaven.

Check the statement that most accurately describes you.

- ❑ I give freely to honor God and to help others.
- ❑ I don't know the freedom of giving to others.

Review the first key to understanding the Treasure Principle.

God owns ____________. I'm His ________ ___________.

Despite the $8.4 million court judgment in 1989, we never lost our house. While paying me a minimum-wage salary, the ministry owned the books I wrote. And suddenly royalties increased. Our ministry has been able to give away about 90 percent of those royalties to missions, famine relief, and prolife work. Sometimes I think God sells the books just to raise funds for ministries close to His heart!

Check the blessings your current giving brings to your life.

❑ Joy ❑ Closeness to God ❑ Freedom

Giving infuses life with joy. It interjects an eternal dimension into the most ordinary day. You couldn't pay me enough not to give. But as great as it is, our present joy isn't the best part!

THE DAY IN REVIEW

Review today's lesson.
What was the most important concept you read today?

____

How will this truth challenge you to be like Christ?

____

____

Pray, asking God to help you give as an act of worship.
Write your prayer below.

____

____

____

____

____

Eternal Rewards

day 4

Yesterday we focused on the rewards giving brings on earth. Today we will look heavenward.

If you imagine heaven as a place where you will strum a harp in endless tedium, you probably dread it. But if you trust Scripture, you will be filled with joy and excitement as you anticipate your heavenly home. Heaven will be not only a place of rest and relief from the burdens of sin and suffering but also a place of great learning, activity, artistic expression, exploration, discovery, camaraderie, and service.

God grants us eternal rewards for doing good works while we are on earth. He doesn't give these rewards equally to everyone:

HE WILL REPAY EACH ONE ACCORDING TO HIS WORKS. *ROMANS 2:6*

WHATEVER GOOD EACH ONE DOES, SLAVE OR FREE, HE WILL RECEIVE THIS BACK FROM THE LORD. *EPHESIANS 6:8*

What is the common theme in these verses?

___

The verses say that God will repay according to our works. One of those works is generous giving. Recall Jesus' encounter with the rich young man, which we studied in week 1. Jesus told him to " 'go, sell your belongings and give to the poor, and you will have treasure in heaven' " (Matt. 19:21). But the man "went away grieving, because he had many possessions" (Matt. 19:22).

Do you think the young man had any idea what he missed? Not only did he forgo an abundant life on earth, but he also missed out on joy in heaven.

Jesus keeps track of our smallest acts of kindness:

WHOEVER GIVES JUST A CUP OF COLD WATER TO ONE OF THESE LITTLE ONES BECAUSE HE IS A DISCIPLE—I ASSURE YOU: HE WILL NEVER LOSE HIS REWARD! *MATTHEW 10:42*

Our instinct is to give to those who will give us something in return. But Jesus told us to give to " 'poor, maimed, lame, or blind. … And you will be blessed, because they cannot repay you; for you will be repaid at the resurrection of the righteous' " (Luke 14:13-14). If we give to those who can't reward us, Christ guarantees that He will personally reward us in heaven.

God keeps a record of all we do for Him, including our giving:

AT THAT TIME THOSE WHO FEARED THE LORD SPOKE TO ONE ANOTHER. THE LORD TOOK NOTICE AND LISTENED. SO A BOOK OF REMEMBRANCE WAS WRITTEN BEFORE HIM FOR THOSE WHO FEARED YAHWEH AND HAD HIGH REGARD FOR HIS NAME. *MALACHI 3:16*

Imagine a scribe in heaven recording each of your gifts on that scroll. The bike you gave to the neighbor kid; the books to prisoners; the monthly checks to the church, missionaries, and pregnancy center—all are being chronicled. Scrolls are made to be read. I look forward to hearing your giving stories and meeting those touched by what you gave.

What are some good works that the scribe will record for you?

____

____

If we cling to what isn't ours, we forgo the opportunity to be granted ownership in heaven. But by generously distributing God's property on earth, we will become property owners in heaven. Now that's something to get excited about!

Many benefits of our present giving will come to us in heaven. Jesus emphasized this in His parable of the dishonest, or shrewd, manager. This guy was in a panic. Accused of squandering his boss's possessions, he risked losing his job.

Read Luke 16:1-13 in your Bible. Was the manager fit to hold another position? ❑ Yes ❑ No

He wasn't strong enough to dig, and he was ashamed to beg. Yet he wanted to be welcomed into the homes of others after he was removed from management. He had an idea to make the situation right with two of his master's debtors.

Write what each debt was reduced to.

_____ measures of oil were reduced to _____.

_____ measures of wheat were reduced to _____.

The master was pleased with his manager's actions.

What does Jesus' parable mean for our giving? Jesus told His followers to use the means of unrighteous money (earthly resources) to make friends (by making a difference in their lives on earth). The reason? " 'So that when it is gone [when life on earth is over], you will be welcomed into eternal dwellings' " (v. 9, NIV).

Our friends in heaven will be those whose lives we've touched on earth, who will have their own eternal dwellings. Luke 16:9 seems to say that our friends' eternal dwellings are places where we stay and fellowship, perhaps as we move about the heavenly kingdom. The money we give to help others on earth will open doors of fellowship with them in heaven. John Bunyan wrote, "Whatever good thing thou dost for him, if done according to the Word, it is … laid up for thee as treasure in chests and coffers, to be brought out to be rewarded before both men and angels, to thy eternal comfort."[1]

Is this a biblical concept? Absolutely! Paul spoke about the Philippians' financial giving and explained, "Not that I seek the gift, but I seek the fruit that is increasing to your account" (Phil. 4:17). God keeps an account open for us in heaven, and every gift given for His glory is a deposit in that account. Not only God, not only others, but also we are the eternal beneficiaries of our giving. Have you been making regular deposits?

What does your giving indicate about your rewards?

Minimal rewards — Some rewards — Abundant rewards

Maybe you're thinking, *Isn't it wrong to be motivated by reward?* No, it isn't. If it were wrong, Christ wouldn't offer it to us as a motivation. Reward is His idea, not ours.

Write the Treasure Principle.

____

Because we give, eternity will be different—for others and for us.

THE DAY IN REVIEW

Review today's lesson.
What was the most important concept you read today?

____

How will this truth challenge you to be like Christ?

____

Pray about your giving. Ask God to motivate you to give more to others. Write your prayer below.

____

____

____

____

Heart Deposits

day 5

Have you heard the song "Thank You (for Giving to the Lord)" by Ray Boltz? It describes our meeting people in heaven who explain how our giving changed their lives. Whether we teach Sunday School or put money in the offering plate, people will one day express their gratitude to us for our giving.

God promises us generous heavenly rewards.

Read Revelation 21:1-6 in your Bible and fill in the blanks.
There will be a new ______________ and a new _________.
We will live with _________________.
There will be no more ______________, ______________,
_________________, or _______________.

The magnificent new heaven and new earth will no longer be under the curse and will be free of suffering. We'll forever be with the person we were made for—Jesus—in a place made for us—heaven.

Nevertheless, many Christians dread the thought of leaving this world. Why? Because so many have collected treasures on earth, not in heaven. Each day brings us closer to death. If your treasures are on earth, that means each day brings you closer to losing your treasures.

John Wesley once toured a vast estate with the proud owner. After riding their horses for hours, they had seen only a fraction of the man's property. At the end of the day when they sat down to dinner, the owner eagerly asked, "Well, Mr. Wesley, what do you think?"

Wesley replied, "I think you're going to have a hard time leaving all this."

What biblical character does this estate owner remind you of?

____

Yes, he and the rich young man had something in common: they placed a very high value on their earthly treasures.

In contrast, I once spoke with Laverne, a woman with terminal cancer. She was crying, not because she was dying but because I asked her to talk about giving. Through tears she said: "Giving melts me. It blows me away to know that God has chosen me to give. It won't be long before I see Him face-to-face. I just want to hear Him say, 'Well done, My good and faithful servant.' " Suddenly Laverne laughed. "I mean, what else matters?" she said. "Why should I care about anything else?"

Laverne's heart was focused on heavenly treasures. Because she was collecting treasures in heaven, each day brought her closer to those treasures.

Laverne embodied an important concept that Jesus taught:

WHERE YOUR TREASURE IS, THERE YOUR HEART WILL BE ALSO. *MATTHEW 6:21*

That's the second key to the Treasure Principle.

My heart always goes where I put God's money.

By telling us that our hearts follow our treasure, Jesus was saying, "Show me your checkbook, your credit-card statement, and your receipts, and I'll show you where your heart is."

Suppose you buy shares of General Motors. What happens? You suddenly develop an interest in GM. You check the financial pages. You see a magazine article about GM and read every word, even though a month ago you would have passed over it.

Suppose you're giving to help African children with AIDS. When you see an article on the subject, you're hooked. If you're sending money to plant churches in India, and an earthquake hits India, you watch the news and pray fervently.

I've heard people say that they want a greater heart for missions. I always respond: "Jesus tells you exactly how to get it. Put your money in missions—and in your church and the poor—and your heart will follow."

God wants your heart. He isn't looking just for donors for His kingdom, those who stand outside the cause and dispassionately consider acts of philanthropy. He's looking for disciples who are immersed in the causes they give to. He wants people who are so filled with a vision for eternity that they wouldn't dream of not investing their money, time, and prayers where they will matter most.

Indicate whether your investments in each of the following areas are making deposits on earth or in heaven.

	On Earth	In Heaven
Money	❑	❑
Possessions	❑	❑
Time	❑	❑
Ministry/service	❑	❑
Prayer	❑	❑
Acts of kindness	❑	❑
Missions	❑	❑
Skills/gifts/abilities	❑	❑

Do your responses indicate that God has your heart?

❑ Yes ❑ No

Moses left Egypt's treasures "since his attention was on the reward" (Heb. 11:26). Can you imagine being that focused on heaven? Someone who spends his life moving away from his treasures has reason to despair. Someone who spends his life moving toward his treasures has reason to rejoice. Are you despairing or rejoicing?

Write the Treasure Principle.

____

____

Write the first key to the Treasure Principle.

Write the second key to the Treasure Principle.

THE DAY IN REVIEW

Review today's lesson.
What was the most important concept you read today?

How will this truth challenge you to be like Christ?

Pray about your response to the activity in the middle of page 48. Ask God to help you focus your heart on heaven by investing in heaven while you are on earth. Write your prayer below.

[1]John Bunyan, *Paul's Departure and Crown,* in *The Works of John Bunyan,* ed. George Offor (Glasgow: Blackie and Son, 1855), 737.

week 3

Heavenly Treasures

day 1

Investing in Your Home

Last week we learned that Christ commands us to give and offers us heavenly rewards for giving. So why is it so difficult to give?

In our society it's considered normal to keep far more than we give, and the raging current of our culture—and often of our churches—makes it difficult to swim upstream. In addition, certain roadblocks tend to get in the way of our giving:

- Unbelief is a roadblock to giving because if we don't believe that God can and will provide for our needs, we tend to hoard our money instead of giving it away.
- Insecurity makes us think that if we give something away, there will not be enough left for ourselves.
- Pride makes us think that we are the source of our provision instead of God, so we are reluctant to give away our resources.
- Idolatry is worshiping and serving anything other than God. Material things become idols when we value them so much that we don't use and give them according to God's purposes.

- The desire for power and control refuses to acknowledge God's ownership and causes us to use money for selfish purposes instead of kingdom purposes.

Go back and circle roadblocks that keep you from giving.

Although these roadblocks are formidable, the greatest deterrent to giving is the illusion that earth is our home. This leads us to the third key to the Treasure Principle:

Heaven, not earth, is my home.

Perhaps it would help if we thought of ourselves as ambassadors to earth rather than permanent residents. An ambassador represents his or her group to another entity. For example, the United Nations comprises ambassadors from 191 countries, who speak for the citizens of their home countries. Although these representatives live in the United States, where the United Nations is headquartered, they are not citizens of this country. Similarly, Christians are ambassadors who represent our true home, heaven:

We are ambassadors for Christ; certain that God is appealing through us, we plead on Christ's behalf, "Be reconciled to God."
2 Corinthians 5:20

Whom do we represent as ambassadors? ________________

Hebrews 11:13 says we are pilgrims, strangers, aliens on earth:

These all died in faith without having received the promises, but they saw them from a distance, greeted them, and confessed that they were foreigners and temporary residents on the earth.

Although this earth can be nice, we are citizens of heaven:

THEY NOW ASPIRE TO A BETTER LAND—A HEAVENLY ONE. THEREFORE GOD IS NOT ASHAMED TO BE CALLED THEIR GOD, FOR HE HAS PREPARED A CITY FOR THEM. *HEBREWS 11:16*

Underline who has prepared this heavenly place for us.

So where we choose to collect our treasures largely depends on where we think our home is.

If heaven is your home, which of the following are true?

- ❑ I will invest in other people.
- ❑ I will collect treasures on earth.
- ❑ I will use my abilities to get rich.
- ❑ I will work to build God's kingdom.
- ❑ I will share the gospel and make disciples.
- ❑ I will invest in my future before sharing with others.

Suppose your home is in France and you are visiting America for three months. You are living in a hotel, and you are told that you can't take anything back to France on your flight home. But you can earn money and mail deposits to your bank in France. Would you fill your hotel room with expensive furniture and wall hangings? Of course not. You would send your money where your home is. You would spend only what you needed on the temporary residence, sending your treasures ahead so that they would be waiting for you when you got home.

Jesus is a builder by trade. He's also omniscient and omnipotent, qualities that are very useful on a building project! Don't you think that the home He's been building for us the past two thousand years is something incredible? Although we've never been to this home, it's the place we were made for, the place made for us. I look forward to seeing my heavenly home.

Heaven, not earth, is your home. How does this realization change the way you view money and possessions?

If we would let the reality sink in that heaven, not earth, is our permanent home, it would forever change the way we think and live. We would stop collecting treasures in our earthly hotel rooms and start sending more ahead to our true home.

Write the Treasure Principle.

Write the third key to the Treasure Principle.

THE DAY IN REVIEW

Review today's lesson.
What was the most important concept you read today?

How will this truth challenge you to be like Christ?

Thank God for the new home that He has designed and built just for you. Ask Him to help your life reflect the truth that heaven, not earth, is your home. Write your prayer below.

Investing Your Life

day 2

Take a ride with me to an isolated place. After a few miles we turn off the road, pass through a gate, and fall in line behind some pickup trucks. They are filled with computers, stereo systems, furniture, appliances, fishing gear, and toys.

Higher and higher we climb until we reach a parking lot. There the drivers unload their cargo. Curious, you watch a man hoist a computer. He staggers to the corner of the lot, then hurls his computer over the edge.

Now you've got to find out what's happening. You scramble out of the car and peer over the edge. At the bottom of the cliff is a giant pit filled with … stuff.

Finally you understand. This is a landfill, a junkyard—the final resting place for the things in our lives.

Sooner or later, everything we own ends up here. Cars, boats, and hot tubs. Clothes, stereos, and barbecue grills. Christmas and birthday presents. The treasures that children quarreled about, friendships were lost over, honesty was sacrificed for, and marriages broke up over—all end up here. (I recommend taking a family field trip to a junkyard. It's a powerful object lesson.)

Have you ever seen the bumper sticker that says, "He who dies with the most toys wins"?

Do you agree or disagree with that statement?

❑ Agree ❑ Disagree

If you disagree, rewrite the statement to make it true.

____

____

Millions of people act as if that bumper sticker were true. The truth is that he who dies with the most toys still dies—and doesn't take his toys with him. When we die after devoting our lives to acquiring things, we don't win. We lose. We move into eternity, but our toys stay behind, filling junkyards. The bumper sticker couldn't be more wrong.

Our lives have two phases: one a dot, the other a line extending from that dot.

Life on earth | Life in heaven

Our present life on earth is the dot. It begins. It ends. It's brief, but from that dot extends a line that goes on forever. That line is eternity, which Christians will spend in heaven.

List some events that complete your dot—your life on earth. Start with categories like your birth, graduation(s), marriage, births of children, first home, jobs, and so on. Then add other significant events.

_______________ _______________

_______________ _______________

_______________ _______________

_______________ _______________

_______________ _______________

_______________ _______________

_______________ _______________

This list isn't comprehensive; we could continue adding significant events in our earthly lives. No matter how long the list, though, we must remember that our time here is brief. We can't record the ending date yet, but it will come one day. At that point our lives will continue on the line of eternity.

This brings us to our fourth key to the Treasure Principle:

I should live not for the dot but for the line.

Someone who lives for the dot lives for treasures that end up in junkyards. Someone who lives for the line lives for treasures that will never end.

Jim Elliot is someone who lived for the line. While a student at Wheaton College in the 1950s, Jim corresponded with a former missionary to Ecuador. Through this correspondence he knew that God was calling him to preach the gospel to an unreached tribe, the Aucas.

In Autumn 1955 missionary pilot Nate Saint spotted an Auca village. During the ensuing months Elliot and several fellow missionaries dropped gifts from a plane, attempting to befriend the hostile tribe.

In January 1956 Elliot and four companions landed on a beach of the Curaray River in eastern Ecuador. They had several friendly contacts with the fierce tribe that had previously killed several Shell Oil company employees. Two days later, however, warriors from the Auca tribe brutally murdered all five men.

Although tragic, that's not the end of the story. Here's where the heavenly treasures come in. Many Aucas eventually came to accept Christ when Jim's wife, Elisabeth, bravely returned to share Christ with those who had killed her husband. Elisabeth's book, *Shadow of the Almighty,* chronicles the life and ministry of a man who knew what it means to collect treasures in heaven, to live for the line and not for the dot.

Giving is living for the line. This is what Jim Elliot was talking about when he said, "He is no fool who gives what he cannot keep to gain what he cannot lose."[1] If you hear those words and think, *Oh, he was one of those superspiritual missionary types who didn't think about gain,* then you are missing the point. Gain was precisely what Jim Elliot was thinking about! He just wanted the kind of gain he couldn't lose. He wanted his treasures to be in heaven.

Check the true statement.

❑ Living for the line means that you must die for your faith.
❑ Living for the line means investing your life in eternity.

Please don't misunderstand this point. You don't have to die for your faith to collect treasures in heaven! However, Jim risked his life to put treasures in heaven. He considered what he had on earth of much less value than the treasures he would possess forever. Jim lived not for the dot but for the line.

Write the fourth key to the Treasure Principle.

____

If God audited your finances, would He conclude that you live more for ☐ the dot or ☐ the line?

What evidence would lead to that conclusion?

____

____

____

THE DAY IN REVIEW

Review today's lesson.
What was the most important concept you read today?

____

____

How will this truth challenge you to be like Christ?

____

____

Pray and ask God to show you what you need to do to live for the line. Ask Him to empower you to make any needed changes. Write your prayer below.

____

____

____

____

____

____

Does Money Buy Happiness?

day 3

A PBS television program called "Affluenza" addresses what it calls the modern-day plague of materialism. The program claims:

- The average American shops six hours a week but spends only 40 minutes playing with his or her children.
- By age 20 we've seen one million commercials.
- Recently, more Americans declared bankruptcy than graduated from college.
- In 90 percent of divorce cases, arguments about money play a prominent role.

Do you think materialism makes Americans happy?

❑ Yes ❑ No

What strikes me about this program is that it doesn't argue against materialism on a moral basis but on a pragmatic one: material wealth doesn't make us happy.

Read the comments of some of the wealthiest people of their day:

- "The care of $200 million is enough to kill anyone. There is no pleasure in it."—W. H. Vanderbilt
- "I am the most miserable man on earth."—John Jacob Astor
- "I have made many millions, but they have brought me no happiness."—John D. Rockefeller
- "Millionaires seldom smile."—Andrew Carnegie
- "I was happier when doing a mechanic's job."—Henry Ford

Perhaps you've heard of lottery winners who are more miserable after winning than they were before. The wealth they dreamed would bring them happiness didn't. Not even close.

Name something you bought that you thought would make you happy but didn't.

Nanci and I have lived in our house for 23 years. For the first nine years it had ugly, orange carpet. We never cared what happened to it. The day we finally installed new carpet, someone lit a candle. The match head fell off and burned a hole in the carpet. The day before we wouldn't have cared. Now we were upset. Were we better off with our nice, new possession?

Every item we buy is one more thing to think about, talk about, clean, repair, rearrange, fret over, and replace when it goes bad. Let's say I get a television for free. Now what? I hook up the antenna or subscribe to a cable service. I buy a new VCR or DVD player. I rent movies. I get surround-sound speakers. I buy a recliner so that I can watch my programs in comfort. All of this costs money. It also takes time, energy, and attention.

The time I devote to my TV and its accessories means less time for communicating with my family, reading God's Word, praying, opening our home to others, or ministering to the needy. My free television is not really free.

In fact, acquiring a possession can influence you to redefine your priorities. At the end of the movie *Schindler's List* is a heart-wrenching scene in which Oskar Schindler, who bought the lives of many Jews from the Nazis, looks at his car and his gold pin and regrets that he didn't give more of his money and possessions to save more lives. Schindler had used his opportunity far better than most. But in the end he longed for a chance to go back and make better choices.

Name two of your possessions that take time and resources away from pursuits that would benefit God's kingdom.

1. ______________________________

2. ______________________________

Unbelievers have no second chance to relive their lives, this time choosing Christ. But Christians also don't get a second chance to live life over, this time doing more to help the needy and invest in God's kingdom. We have one brief opportunity—a lifetime on earth—to use our resources to make a difference.

Five minutes after we die, we'll know exactly how we should have lived.

Five minutes after you die, what will you wish you had given away while you still had the chance?

____

Why not give away the items now? Why not spend the rest of your life closing the gap between what you are giving and what you will wish you had given?

Will you commit to giving this away now? ☐ Yes ☐ No
If not, why not?

____

Reflect on the events you identified in day 2 that make up your dot (see p. 55). Now write your own obituary, based solely on those events.

____

____

____

____

____

____

How do you feel about what you've written?

____

Write your obituary again, this time from heaven's perspective. What have you done that has eternal value?

____

____

____

____

____

____

Do you think God is pleased with your earthly life?
❑ Yes ❑ No

Has your focus been on the dot or the line? ______________

Maybe your life is Christ-centered, with few regrets. Maybe you're daily collecting treasures in heaven.

Or maybe not. If you're like me, you wish heaven's summary of your life were more pleasing to the Audience of One. You may be discouraged by what you've written. If so, don't lose hope. The good news is that while you're still here, you have an opportunity, with God's empowerment, to edit your life and thereby your obituary to make an eternal difference.

THE DAY IN REVIEW

Review today's lesson.
What was the most important concept you read today?

____

____

How will this truth challenge you to be like Christ?

____

____

Examine the way you have answered today's activities. Pray, confessing that money and possessions don't satisfy and asking God to help you live a life that makes an eternal difference. Write your prayer below.

____

____

____

____

____

____

Profit or Loss?

day 4

As I write this, the winds are horrendous. I'm not sure how fast they are spinning, but tumbleweeds are flying, adding prickly barricades to our fence lines. If I tried to keep hold of something outside, it would be futile. The wind gives me a new perspective on what Solomon called "a pursuit of the wind":

WHEN I CONSIDERED ALL THAT I HAD ACCOMPLISHED AND WHAT I HAD LABORED TO ACHIEVE, I FOUND EVERYTHING TO BE FUTILE AND A PURSUIT OF THE WIND. THERE WAS NOTHING TO BE GAINED UNDER THE SUN. *ECCLESIASTES 2:11*

Solomon was the wealthiest man on earth, but he learned that affluence doesn't satisfy. All it does is create greater opportunities to chase mirages. People tend to run out of money before mirages, so they cling to the myth that things they can't afford will satisfy them. Solomon's money never ran out. He tried everything, saying:

ALL THAT MY EYES DESIRED, I DID NOT DENY THEM. I DID NOT REFUSE MYSELF ANY PLEASURE, FOR I TOOK PLEASURE IN ALL MY STRUGGLES. THIS WAS MY REWARD FOR ALL MY STRUGGLES. *ECCLESIASTES 2:10*

Written by someone who had tried it all, the Book of Ecclesiastes shows us the good, the bad, and the ugly of money.

Read Ecclesiastes 5:10-15 in your Bible.
Then, on the following page, match each verse on the left with its paraphrase on the right.

___ 1. "The one who loves money is never satisfied with money."

___ 2. "Whoever loves wealth is never satisfied with income."

___ 3. "When good things increase, the ones who consume multiply."

___ 4. "What is the profit to the owner except to gaze at them with his eyes?"

___ 5. "The sleep of the worker is sweet, whether he eats little or much; but the abundance of the rich permits him no sleep."

___ 6. "There is a sickening tragedy I have seen under the sun: wealth kept by its owner to his harm."

___ 7. "That wealth was lost in a bad venture."

___ 8. "As he came from his mother's womb, so he will go again, naked as he came; he will take nothing for his efforts that he can carry in his hands."

a. The more you have, the more you have to lose.

b. The more you have, the more you have to worry about.

c. The more you have, the more people will come after it.

d. The more you have, the more you want.

e. The more you have, the more you realize it does you no good.

f. The more you have, the more you'll leave behind.

g. The more you have, the less you're satisfied.

h. The more you have, the more you can hurt yourself by holding on to it.

Verse 15 seems to summarize the passage as well as the entire Book of Ecclesiastes. It should remind you of the Treasure Principle. Complete the principle.

You can't take it ________ ________,

but you can ________ ____ ____ ______________.

Why do you think we keep getting fooled into thinking that things will satisfy?

____

We keep pursuing the wind because our hearts yearn for treasure here and now. We are tempted to imagine that the earthly treasures we see around us are the genuine items rather than mere shadows of the real treasures.

Check one of the following.

- ❑ I have a habit of pursuing material things because I think they will satisfy.
- ❑ I seek only the things I need or things I use to help others.

Let's look at a parable Jesus told about treasures.

Read Luke 12:13-21 in your Bible.
Whom was Jesus addressing?

____

What was Jesus' warning in verse 15?

- ❑ Life equals the stuff you have.
- ❑ Your life isn't in the abundance of your possessions.
- ❑ The one with the most toys wins.

What did God call the rich man?

❑ A fool ❑ A wise man

How did Jesus summarize His parable in verse 21?

" 'That's how it is with the one who stores up treasure for _______________ and is not _______________ toward God.' "

What do you think it means to be rich toward God?

____

____

____

Unlike Solomon, the rich man had not learned the lesson that material things do not satisfy. God saw eternity when the man saw only the things of this earth.

What about you? Are you convinced that only earthly treasures do not satisfy? Check the statement that applies to you.

- ❑ I'm not convinced. I enjoy acquiring things.
- ❑ I'm beginning to realize that things do not satisfy, but I am struggling to change my priorities.
- ❑ I'm absolutely convinced that earthly treasure will never satisfy me.

THE DAY IN REVIEW

Review today's lesson.
What was the most important concept you read today?

____

____

How will this truth challenge you to be like Christ?

____

____

Pray, asking God to bring you to the realization that seeking material possessions is like pursuing the wind. Ask Him to help you change your habits and priorities to focus on heavenly treasures. Write your prayer below.

____

____

____

____

____

____

____

____

True Riches

If affluenza is the disease, what's the cure? If materialism is the poison, what's the antidote? Paul offered an answer.

In the following verse, underline what we are commanded to do.

INSTRUCT THOSE WHO ARE RICH IN THE PRESENT AGE NOT TO BE ARROGANT OR TO SET THEIR HOPE ON THE UNCERTAINTY OF WEALTH, BUT ON GOD, WHO RICHLY PROVIDES US WITH ALL THINGS TO ENJOY. INSTRUCT THEM TO DO GOOD, TO BE RICH IN GOOD WORKS, TO BE GENEROUS, WILLING TO SHARE, STORING UP FOR THEMSELVES A GOOD FOUNDATION FOR THE AGE TO COME, SO THAT THEY MAY TAKE HOLD OF LIFE THAT IS REAL. *1 TIMOTHY 6:17-19*

Notice that Paul brings us right back to the Treasure Principle. When he speaks of giving to "store treasure for themselves a good foundation for the age to come," he's no doubt directly referring to Christ's words in Matthew 6.

Write the Treasure Principle.

____

____

God wants us to use earthly treasures to collect heavenly treasures. Paul said that being generous and willing to share and being rich in good works allow us to "take hold of life that is real." Real as opposed to what? The second-class life of materialism.

Paul's teaching on generosity introduces the fifth key to the Treasure Principle:

Giving is the only antidote to materialism.

The act of giving vividly reminds us that it's all about God, not about us. It says: "I am not the point. He is the point. He does not exist for me. I exist for Him." God's money has a higher purpose than our affluence. Giving is joyful surrender to a greater person and a greater agenda. Giving affirms Christ's lordship. It dethrones us and exalts Him. It breaks the chains of mammon that would enslave us.

Underline the word in each pair that correctly completes the sentence.

(Keeping, giving) something shows that I believe I am the owner.
(Keeping, giving) something shows that I believe God is the owner.

As long as we still have something, we believe we own it. But when we give it away, we relinquish control, power, and prestige. At the moment of release, the light turns on. The spell of materialism is broken. Our minds clear. We recognize God as the owner, ourselves as the servants, and others as the intended beneficiaries of what God has entrusted to us. Giving doesn't strip us of vested interests; rather, it shifts our vested interests from earth to heaven—from self to God.

What can you give besides money to invest in heavenly treasures?

____

____

Of course, money isn't all we can give. Time, wisdom, and expertise are wonderful gifts.

Describe what giving does to change a believer's priorities and perspective.

____

____

____

____

Giving breaks affluenza's fever. Giving breaks us free from the gravitational hold of money and possessions. Giving shifts us to a new center of gravity—heaven.

Have you ever thought about what will happen to the material universes when Christ returns? The Bible tells us,

ON THAT DAY THE HEAVENS WILL PASS AWAY WITH A LOUD NOISE, THE ELEMENTS WILL BURN AND BE DISSOLVED, AND THE EARTH AND THE WORKS ON IT WILL BE DISCLOSED. *2 PETER 3:10*

How does that verse make you feel?

❑ Afraid ❑ Depressed
❑ Peaceful ❑ Hopeful

That verse would be depressing if this world were our home. But it isn't! It would be depressing if we couldn't use our lives and resources to make a difference for eternity. But we can!

C. S. Lewis wrote: "We are halfhearted creatures, fooling about with drink and sex and ambition when infinite joy is offered us, like an ignorant child who wants to go on making mud pies in a slum because he cannot imagine what is meant by the offer of a holiday at sea. We are far too easily pleased."[2] Even many Christians have settled for a life spent acquiring unsatisfying material possessions, like making mud pies in a slum. There's something so much better than anything the world can offer—the treasures of eternal investments and exhilarating joy. And giving holds the key to those treasures.

Place an *X* beside things you are already giving. Place a check mark beside things you would like to start giving.

❑ Money ❑ Talents
❑ Skills ❑ Spiritual gifts
❑ Wisdom ❑ Knowledge
❑ Encouragement ❑ Time

Write the first five keys to the Treasure Principle.

1. ______________________________
2. ______________________________
3. ______________________________
4. ______________________________
5. ______________________________

THE DAY IN REVIEW

Review today's lesson.
What was the most important concept you read today?

____

____

How will this truth challenge you to be like Christ?

____

____

____

Pray and confess that giving is the only antidote to materialism. Express your desire to collect treasures in heaven. Ask God to help you become more willing to give and find practical ways to do so.

____

____

____

____

____

____

____

____

[1]Elisabeth Elliot, *Shadow of the Almighty: The Life and Testament of Jim Elliot* (New York: Harper and Brothers, 1958), 15.
[2]C. S. Lewis, *The Weight of Glory* (New York: Macmillan, 1949), 2.

week 4

Collecting Treasures

day 1

Your Initial Investment

Sam Houston was a soldier and politician who helped Texas win independence from Mexico in the 1800s. He was the first president of the Republic of Texas and then became its governor in 1859.

To everyone's amazement Houston came to Christ. After his baptism Houston said he wanted to pay half the local minister's salary. When someone asked him why, he responded, "My pocketbook was baptized too."

Like Sam Houston, you may understand that giving is an inseparable part of living the Christian life. But you might be wondering, *Where do I start?* A logical place is where God started His Old Covenant children.

EVERY TENTH OF THE LAND'S PRODUCE, GRAIN FROM THE SOIL OR FRUIT FROM THE TREES, BELONGS TO THE LORD; IT IS HOLY TO THE LORD.
LEVITICUS 27:30

Circle the word *tenth* in the preceding Scripture.

Another word for *tenth* is *tithe.* God said that 10 percent, or the tithe, was to be given back to Him. Freewill offerings were optional, but the 10 percent was mandatory.

What were the people supposed to tithe?

____

The people were required to give a tenth of the land's produce, grain from the soil, or fruit from the trees. Why? Because it belonged to the Lord. Proverbs 3:9 says,

HONOR THE LORD WITH YOUR POSSESSIONS
AND WITH THE FIRST PRODUCE OF YOUR ENTIRE HARVEST.

What do you think is the significance of the word *first?*

____

God's children give to Him first, not last. They give to Him from the first of what they have, not what's left over.

When God's children weren't giving as they should, He said,

"WILL A MAN ROB GOD? YET YOU ARE ROBBING ME!"

YOU ASK: "HOW DO WE ROB YOU?"

"BY NOT MAKING THE PAYMENTS OF 10 PERCENT AND THE CONTRIBUTIONS. YOU ARE SUFFERING UNDER A CURSE, YET YOU—THE WHOLE NATION—ARE STILL ROBBING ME. BRING THE FULL 10 PERCENT INTO THE STOREHOUSE SO THAT THERE MAY BE FOOD IN MY HOUSE. TEST ME IN THIS WAY," SAYS THE LORD OF HOSTS. "SEE IF I WILL NOT OPEN THE FLOODGATES OF HEAVEN AND POUR OUT A BLESSING FOR YOU WITHOUT MEASURE." *MALACHI 3:8-10*

God said that if we don't give to Him, we are robbing or stealing from Him.

Jesus validated the mandatory tithe, even on small things:

WOE TO YOU, SCRIBES AND PHARISEES, HYPOCRITES! YOU PAY A TENTH OF MINT, DILL, AND CUMIN, YET YOU HAVE NEGLECTED THE MORE IMPORTANT MATTERS OF THE LAW—JUSTICE, MERCY, AND FAITH. THESE THINGS SHOULD HAVE BEEN DONE WITHOUT NEGLECTING THE OTHERS. *MATTHEW 23:23*

What were the scribes and Pharisees willing to give?

- ❑ Their hearts
- ❑ A tenth of mint, dill, and cumin
- ❑ A tenth of their possessions

What were they neglecting?

- ❑ Their duties
- ❑ The tithe
- ❑ Justice, mercy, and faith

How did Jesus respond?

- ❑ They should neglect the tithe of mint, dill, and cumin.
- ❑ They should give attention only to justice, mercy, and faith.
- ❑ They should give attention to all of these.

Jesus said that both kinds of giving were important. The scribes and Pharisees should have given the tenth of mint, dill, and cumin without neglecting justice, mercy, and faith.

The Bible doesn't give another word about tithing after the Gospels. It's neither commanded nor rescinded, and Christians heatedly debate whether tithing is still a starting place for giving. I have mixed feelings on this issue. I detest legalism. I certainly don't want to try to pour new wine into old wineskins, imposing superseded First Covenant restrictions on Christians. Every New Testament example of giving goes far beyond the tithe. However, none falls short of it. The church fathers Origen, Jerome, and Augustine taught that the tithe is the minimal giving requirement for Christians.

A timeless truth lies behind the concept of giving God our firstfruits. Whether or not the tithe is still the minimal measure of those firstfruits, I ask myself, *Does God expect His New Covenant children to give less than His Old Covenant children?*

How would you answer that question?

❑ Yes ❑ No

Why or why not?

___

___

___

It seems fair to ask, "God, do You expect less of believers today—who have Your Holy Spirit and live in the wealthiest society in human history—than You demanded of the poorest Israelite?"

A recent Barna research report indicates that only 7 percent of born-again adults tithe to a church. The amount of gross income that born-again adults give to a church averages 3.8 percent. Eighteen percent of born-again adults give no money to a church at all.[1]

Isn't it troubling that in this wealthy society, giving amounts to a small fraction of the First Covenant standard? Whatever we are teaching about giving today, either it's not true to Scripture, the message isn't getting through, or we're being disobedient.

Do you tithe by giving a tenth of your income to God's work?

❑ Yes ❑ No

Why or why not? ___

___

___

The tithe is God's historical method to get us on the path of giving. In that sense, it can serve as a gateway to the joy of grace giving—giving beyond the tithe. It's unhealthy to view tithing as a place to stop, but it can still be a good place to start. Tithing isn't the ceiling of giving; it's the floor. It's not the finish line of giving; it's just the starting block. Tithing can be the training wheels to launch us into the mind-set, skills, and habits of grace giving.

Write the Treasure Principle.

____

How does tithing help you collect treasures in heaven?

____

____

____

THE DAY IN REVIEW

Review today's lesson.
What was the most important concept you read today?

____

How will this truth challenge you to be like Christ?

____

____

Pray about the amount you are giving. Ask God what He wants you to give. Write your prayer below.

____

____

____

____

____

____

Blessed by Giving

day 2

In the passage we studied yesterday from Malachi, God said that the Israelites robbed Him by withholding not only their mandatory tithes but also their voluntary contributions above the tithe (see Mal. 3:8). Paul encouraged voluntary giving:

EACH PERSON SHOULD DO AS HE HAS DECIDED IN HIS HEART—NOT OUT OF REGRET OR OUT OF NECESSITY, FOR GOD LOVES A CHEERFUL GIVER. *2 CORINTHIANS 9:7*

What does *cheerful giving* mean?

____

____

God wants us to love Him so much that we freely give to Him from that love—both the tithe and freewill offerings.

Even when our offerings are above the tithe, God has expectations for us. To give less than He expects of us is to rob Him.

Circle the word *obedience* as you read the following verse.

THROUGH THE PROOF OF THIS SERVICE, THEY WILL GLORIFY GOD FOR YOUR OBEDIENCE TO THE CONFESSION OF THE GOSPEL OF CHRIST, AND FOR YOUR GENEROSITY IN SHARING WITH THEM AND WITH OTHERS. *2 CORINTHIANS 9:13*

Of course, God doesn't expect us all to give the same amount. We are to give in proportion to how He has blessed us.

Read Deuteronomy 16:10,16-17 in your Bible.
How are we to give? Fill in the blanks.

In proportion to ______________________________
Suited ____________________________________
According to the ______________________________

Some decide to start giving by saying: "We'll take this gradually. We'll start with 5 percent." But that's like saying, "I used to rob six convenience stores a year. This year, by God's grace, I'll rob only three." The point is not to rob God less. It's not to rob God at all.

True, some people would sacrifice more by giving 5 percent of their incomes than others would by tithing or giving even 50 or 90 percent. Certainly, the affluent should not assume that 10 percent automatically fulfills their obligation. The 90 percent belongs to God too. He doesn't look at just what we give. He also looks at what we keep.

What percent of your income are you giving to God? _____

I've had the privilege of interviewing many people who are cheerful givers. The great majority mention tithing as the practice that first stretched them to give more. They tithed and then watched God provide. Their hearts grew in devotion to His kingdom. Now years later they're giving 60, 80, or even 95 percent of their incomes! But it was tithing that set them on the road to giving.

Look at the results of tithing in obedience.

"BRING THE FULL 10 PERCENT INTO THE STOREHOUSE SO THAT THERE MAY BE FOOD IN MY HOUSE. TEST ME IN THIS WAY," SAYS THE LORD OF HOSTS. "SEE IF I WILL NOT OPEN THE FLOODGATES OF HEAVEN AND POUR OUT A BLESSING FOR YOU WITHOUT MEASURE." *MALACHI 3:10*

What are the results of tithing?

- ❑ There will be food in God's house.
- ❑ None. God is just testing your obedience.
- ❑ God will open the floodgates of heaven.
- ❑ God will pour out blessing without measure.

Ironically, many people can't afford to give precisely because they are not giving.

Read Haggai 1:9-11 in your Bible.
What were the consequences of not giving?

____

____

The people experienced a drought and lost their crops and animals. If we pay our debt to God first, then we will incur His blessing to help us pay our debts to people. But when we rob God to pay people, we rob ourselves of God's blessing. No wonder we don't have enough. It's a vicious cycle, and it takes obedient faith to break out of it.

When people tell me they can't afford to tithe, I ask them, "If your income were reduced by 10 percent, would you die?" They say, 'No.' And I say, "Then you've admitted that you can afford to tithe. You just don't want to."

I'm not saying that it's easy to give. I'm saying that it's much easier to live on 90 percent or 50 percent or 10 percent of your income *inside* God's will than it is to live on 100 percent of your income *outside* God's will.

Tithing is like a toddler's first steps. They aren't his last or best steps, but they're a good start. Once you learn to ride a bike, you don't need training wheels. Once you learn to give, tithing becomes irrelevant. And if you can ride the bike without ever using training wheels, good for you.

I have no problem with people who say, "We're not under the tithe," just as long as they're not using that to justify giving less. But in my mind the current giving statistics among

Christians clearly indicate that most of us need a giving jump-start. If you find a gateway to giving that's better than the tithe, wonderful. But if not, why not start where God started His First Covenant children?

The apostle Paul told the Corinthians about a group of generous, obedient believers in Macedonia:

DURING A SEVERE TESTING BY AFFLICTION, THEIR ABUNDANCE OF JOY AND THEIR DEEP POVERTY OVERFLOWED INTO THE WEALTH OF THEIR GENEROSITY. I TESTIFY THAT, ON THEIR OWN, ACCORDING TO THEIR ABILITY AND BEYOND THEIR ABILITY, THEY BEGGED US INSISTENTLY FOR THE PRIVILEGE OF SHARING IN THE MINISTRY TO THE SAINTS. *2 CORINTHIANS 8:2-4*

Paul challenged the Corinthians also to excel in the grace of giving:

NOW AS YOU EXCEL IN EVERYTHING—IN FAITH, IN SPEECH, IN KNOWLEDGE, IN ALL DILIGENCE, AND IN YOUR LOVE FOR US—EXCEL ALSO IN THIS GRACE. *2 CORINTHIANS 8:7*

Scott Lewis attended a conference in which Bill Bright challenged people to give one million dollars to help fulfill the Great Commission. This amount was laughable to Scott—far beyond anything he could imagine—because his machinery business was generating an income of under $50,000 a year.

Bill asked, "How much did you give last year?" Scott felt pretty good about his answer: "We gave $17,000, about 35 percent of our income."

Without blinking an eye, Bill responded, "Over the next year why don't you set a goal to give $50,000?"

Scott thought Bill hadn't understood. That was more than he had made all year! But Scott and his wife decided to trust God with Bill's challenge, asking Him to do the impossible.

God provided in amazing ways. With a miraculous December 31 provision, the Lewises were able to give $50,000. The next year they set a goal of giving $100,000. And again God provided.

Scott told me that in 2001 they passed the one-million-dollar mark in their giving. The best part is that they aren't stopping. That's what it means to excel at giving.

Check one of the following.

- ❑ I'm not ready to tithe, but I commit to pray about this decision.
- ❑ I commit to obey God by starting or continuing to tithe.
- ❑ I commit to excel at giving by moving beyond the tithe.

THE DAY IN REVIEW

Review today's lesson.
What was the most important concept you read today?

____
____

How will this truth challenge you to be like Christ?

____
____
____

Pray about your response to the final activity in today's lesson. Seek God's will for your giving. Record your prayer below.

____
____
____
____
____
____
____
____

Real Returns

day 3

People ask, "Should I give now, or should I hang on to it, hoping my investments will do well and I'll have more to give in a year or two?"

I respond with two questions of my own: "How soon do you want to experience God's blessing?" and "Do you want to be sure the money goes to God's kingdom, or are you willing to risk that it won't?" When we stand before God, I don't believe He will say, "You blew it when you gave Me all that money before the stock market peaked." I don't believe it's ever wrong to give now.

In the following verse, underline the return on our investment with Jesus. Circle our inheritance.

EVERYONE WHO HAS LEFT HOUSES, BROTHERS OR SISTERS, FATHER OR MOTHER, CHILDREN, OR FIELDS BECAUSE OF MY NAME WILL RECEIVE 100 TIMES MORE AND WILL INHERIT ETERNAL LIFE. *MATTHEW 19:29*

That's 10,000 percent interest! Eternal life! God can produce far greater returns on money invested in heaven today than Wall Street or real estate ever can.

We can identify several reasons to give now. First, if we delay, the economy may change, and we'll have less to give later. God's Word says we don't know what's going to happen in the future.

Read James 4:13-17 on page 81 and answer the following statements *T* for *true* or *F* for *false.*

___ If we plan to invest, we'll succeed.

___ We don't know what tomorrow will bring.

___ We will carry out our plans only if God wills them.

___ It's OK to boast about our investments if they seem like a sure thing.

___ Postponing giving can be a sin.

COME NOW, YOU WHO SAY, "TODAY OR TOMORROW WE WILL TRAVEL TO SUCH AND SUCH A CITY AND SPEND A YEAR THERE AND DO BUSINESS AND MAKE A PROFIT." YOU DON'T EVEN KNOW WHAT TOMORROW WILL BRING—WHAT YOUR LIFE WILL BE! FOR YOU ARE A BIT OF SMOKE THAT APPEARS FOR A LITTLE WHILE, THEN VANISHES. INSTEAD, YOU SHOULD SAY, "IF THE LORD WILLS, WE WILL LIVE AND DO THIS OR THAT." BUT AS IT IS, YOU BOAST IN YOUR ARROGANCE. ALL SUCH BOASTING IS EVIL. SO, FOR THE PERSON WHO KNOWS TO DO GOOD AND DOESN'T DO IT, IT IS A SIN. *JAMES 4:13-17*

Countless investors have been sure about getting great returns on money that disappears overnight. A more sure investment is investing in the good that God wants us to do now.

The second reason we must give now is that if we delay, our hearts may change, and we may not follow through with giving. If you procrastinate, the same heart that's prompting you to give today may later persuade you not to. Why? Because when you postpone giving, your heart's vested interests increase on earth and decrease in heaven. Additionally, you might spend the resources you had set aside for the Lord's work on earthly treasures and not have the financial means to give to the Lord when the need is greatest.

The final reason to give now is that if you delay, your life may end before you've given what you intended. You may think: *No problem. I'm putting my church and several ministries in my will.* By all means, give heavily to God's kingdom through estate planning. But what kind of faith does it take to part with your money once you die? You don't have any choice!

Death isn't your best opportunity to give; it's your last opportunity. God rewards acts of faith we do while we are alive.

Name three reasons to give now.

1. ____________________________________
2. ____________________________________
3. ____________________________________

When the Lord returns, what will happen to the money sitting in bank accounts, retirement programs, estates, and foundations? It will burn like wood, hay, and straw, when it could have been exchanged for gold, silver, and precious stones (see 1 Cor. 3:10-15). Money that could have been used to feed the hungry and fulfill the Great Commission will go up in smoke.

What about our children? Aren't we supposed to leave them all our money? No! Nanci and I will leave to our two daughters only enough to be of modest assistance but not enough to change their lifestyles or undercut their need to plan, pray with, and depend on their husbands. They understand and agree with our plan to give most of our estate to God's kingdom.

Leaving a large inheritance to children is not just a missed opportunity to invest in God's kingdom. It's also rarely in the children's best interests.

Check the harmful effects of a large inheritance on children.

- ❑ Promotes unhappiness
- ❑ Makes people more generous
- ❑ Encourages hard work
- ❑ Divides siblings
- ❑ Promotes greed
- ❑ Funds temptations
- ❑ Promotes family unity

Leaving more to God's kingdom and less to financially independent children is not just an act of love toward God but also toward your children.

In Old Testament times leaving an inheritance was critical:

A GOOD MAN LEAVES AN INHERITANCE TO HIS GRANDCHILDREN, BUT THE SINNER'S WEALTH IS STORED UP FOR THE RIGHTEOUS. *PROVERBS 13:22*

At that time children couldn't afford to buy their own land and could end up enslaved or unable to care for their parents. But today inheritances are often windfalls for people who are financially independent and already have more than they need.

Your children should love the Lord, work hard, and experience the joy of trusting God. More important than leaving your children a financial inheritance is leaving them a spiritual heritage. Share with them the good news in 1 Peter 1:3-4:

BLESSED BE THE GOD AND FATHER OF OUR LORD JESUS CHRIST. ACCORDING TO HIS GREAT MERCY, HE HAS GIVEN US A NEW BIRTH INTO A LIVING HOPE THROUGH THE RESURRECTION OF JESUS CHRIST FROM THE DEAD, AND INTO AN INHERITANCE THAT IS IMPERISHABLE, UNCORRUPTED, AND UNFADING, KEPT IN HEAVEN FOR YOU.

Which kind of inheritance do you want for your children?

- ❑ Wood, hay, and straw
- ❑ Imperishable, uncorrupted, and unfading

Let God decide how much to provide for your adult children. Once they're on their own, the money you've generated under God's provision doesn't belong to your children. It belongs to Him. After all, if your money manager died, what would you think if he left all your money to his children?

Check any reasons you have delayed giving.

- ❑ Waiting for investments to earn more
- ❑ Saving it for children

Write any commitments you would like to make as a result of today's lesson.

About giving now: ______________________________

____

About investing more in the kingdom than in your children:

THE DAY IN REVIEW

Review today's lesson.
What was the most important concept you read today?

How will this truth challenge you to be like Christ?

Pray about any commitments you made today and ask for courage to carry them out. Ask God what He wants you to give and to what area of His kingdom. Write your prayer below.

Distributing Wealth

day 4

R. G. LeTourneau, the inventor of earthmoving machines in the early 20th century, created nearly three hundred inventions. He gave away 90 percent of his fortune, but the money came in faster than he could give it away. LeTourneau said, "I shovel it out, and God shovels it back—but God has a bigger shovel!"

Jesus expressed it like this:

GIVE, AND IT WILL BE GIVEN TO YOU; A GOOD MEASURE—PRESSED DOWN, SHAKEN TOGETHER, AND RUNNING OVER—WILL BE POURED INTO YOUR LAP. FOR WITH THE MEASURE YOU USE, IT WILL BE MEASURED BACK TO YOU. *LUKE 6:38*

The more you give, the more comes back to you because God is the greatest giver in the universe, and He won't let you outgive Him. Go ahead and try. See what happens.

Check the statement that is true.

❑ God's blessing is always material wealth.
❑ God's blessing may or may not be material wealth.

The health-and-wealth gospel held by many people today claims that God's blessing always comes in the form of material riches. The more money we give to Him, the more He returns to us. Prosperity theology is built on a half-truth. God often prospers givers materially, but He won't let us treat Him like a no-lose slot machine or a cosmic genie who does our bidding. Giving is a sacrifice, and sometimes we feel that sacrifice.

God has given many believers considerable material blessings. Have you ever asked yourself, *Why has He provided so much?* Paul tells us exactly why God provides more than we need:

THE ONE WHO PROVIDES SEED FOR THE SOWER AND BREAD FOR FOOD WILL PROVIDE AND MULTIPLY YOUR SEED AND INCREASE THE HARVEST OF YOUR RIGHTEOUSNESS, AS YOU ARE ENRICHED IN EVERY WAY FOR ALL GENEROSITY.
2 CORINTHIANS 9:10-11

Paul provides the sixth and final key to the Treasure Principle:

God prospers me not to raise my standard of living but to raise my standard of giving.

Why does God give us more money than we need?

- ❑ So that we can find more ways to spend it
- ❑ So that we can indulge ourselves and spoil our children
- ❑ So that we can give generously
- ❑ So that we don't need to feel a sense of God's provision

God gives us wealth so that we can give. When God provides more money, we often think that it's a blessing. It would be just as scriptural to think that it's a test of how we will use it.

As God's money managers, we have legitimate needs, and the Owner is generous. He doesn't demand that His stewards live in poverty, and He doesn't resent our making reasonable expenditures on ourselves. But suppose the Owner sees us living luxuriously in mansions, driving the best cars, flying first-class, buying expensive clothes and electronic gadgets, and eating at the best restaurants? Isn't there a point when His stewards can cross the line from reasonable expenses to opulence and self-indulgence? Won't the Owner call us to account for squandering money that's not ours? God's servants are told:

IT IS EXPECTED OF MANAGERS THAT EACH ONE BE FOUND FAITHFUL.
1 CORINTHIANS 4:2

We spend the money God has entrusted to us. We don't own the store; we just work here!

Not everyone prospers materially. At the other end of the spectrum are those who don't have enough.

Why do you think God gives some of His children more than they need and others less than they need?

____

____

God distributes wealth unevenly not because He loves some of His children more than others but so that He can use His children to help one another. He doesn't want us to have too little or too much. Consider this perspective:

GIVE ME NEITHER POVERTY NOR WEALTH;
FEED ME WITH THE FOOD I NEED.
OTHERWISE, I MIGHT HAVE TOO MUCH
AND DENY YOU, SAYING, "WHO IS THE LORD?"
OR I MIGHT HAVE NOTHING AND STEAL,
PROFANING THE NAME OF MY GOD. *PROVERBS 30:8-9*

Mark the statements *T* for *true* or *F* for *false*.

___ It's best to have either poverty or wealth.
___ If I were in poverty, I would curse God.
___ If I had to live in poverty, I might steal.
___ If I were wealthy, I would freely give to others.
___ If I were wealthy, I would think too highly of myself.
___ It's best to have just what I need.

Those who prosper materially have the privilege of being part of God's plan when they distribute their wealth to their brothers and sisters on His behalf.

Do you have less or more than you need? ❑ Less ❑ More

Reread 2 Corinthians 9:10-11 on page 86.

Paul said that the God who supplies seed to the sower will increase our store of seed. Why? So that we can stockpile seed or eat it? No, so that we can scatter it and spread it out for it to bear fruit. Abundance isn't God's provision for me to live in luxury. It's His provision for me to help others live. God entrusts me with this money not to build my kingdom on earth but to build His kingdom in heaven.

Write the Treasure Principle.

____

____

Are you eager to plant God's money in the field of a world that needs Christ? ❑ Yes ❑ No
Does the thought of giving to what will count for eternity make your spine tingle? ❑ Yes ❑ No
Does storing up treasures in heaven make your heart leap?
❑ Yes ❑ No

If we understood the out-of-this-world returns, we'd join the Macedonians and beg for the privilege of giving (see 2 Cor. 8:1-5).

Remember that $8.4 million lawsuit? Recently, the 10-year judgment period expired. Our ministry board encouraged us to start taking book royalties again. Nanci and I talked and prayed about it. We decided that we don't need a higher standard of living, a better house or car, a better retirement program or more insurance. So with joy in our hearts we said, "No thanks." Later we discovered that the abortion clinic had the judgment extended for another 10 years. But we're thankful we didn't know that when we made our decision.

They are not our book royalties; they are God's. Nanci and I have a certain amount we live on, and we are comfortable.

The rest goes to the kingdom. God faithfully provides for us. And we get to experience one of life's greatest thrills—the joy of giving.

Write the sixth key to the Treasure Principle.

____

____

Are you willing to give sacrificially to collect treasures in heaven? ❑ Yes ❑ No

If God has prospered you, how will you distribute your resources to others?

____

____

THE DAY IN REVIEW

Review today's lesson.
What was the most important concept you read today?

____

How will this truth challenge you to be like Christ?

____

____

Ask God to raise your standard of giving and to show you new ways He wants you to give. Write your prayer below.

____

____

____

____

____

____

Joyful Giving

day 5

The transformation that giving can bring is graphically portrayed in Charles Dickens's classic story *A Christmas Carol.* When the story begins, Ebenezer Scrooge is wealthy and miserable. He's caustic, complaining, and horrendously greedy. After encounters with three spirits on Christmas Day, he is given a second chance at life.

Read this description of the transformed Scrooge: "He went to church, and walked about the streets, and watched the people hurrying to and fro, and patted children on the head, and questioned beggars, and looked down into the kitchens of houses, and up to the windows; and found that everything could yield him pleasure. He had never dreamed that any walk—that anything—could give him so much happiness."[2]

After his transformation Scrooge walks through the streets of London, freely distributing his wealth to the needy. He who only yesterday had scoffed at the idea of charity now takes his greatest pleasure in giving.

At the end of the story Dickens says of Scrooge: "Some people laughed to see the alteration in him, but he let them laugh, and little heeded them. … His own heart laughed, and that was quite enough for him. … And it was always said of him, that he knew how to keep Christmas well, if any man alive possessed the knowledge."[3]

The source of Scrooge's transformation was gaining an eternal perspective. Through supernatural intervention Scrooge was allowed to see his past, present, and still-changeable future through the eyes of eternity. Let's ask God for the same insight into our lives.

Ebenezer Scrooge leaped for joy on the streets of London because he had discovered the life-giving antidote to the materialism that had poisoned his soul. Scrooge had learned the Treasure Principle—the secret of joyful giving.

Write the Treasure Principle.

____

____

One of Jesus' statements recorded in Acts doesn't appear in the Gospels. Perhaps God added it later to make it stand out:

IT IS MORE BLESSED TO GIVE THAN TO RECEIVE. *ACTS 20:35*

We're so absorbed with getting what's ours that we miss what brings real blessing and joy: giving God what's His. Giving is doing what we were made for: loving God and our neighbors (see Matt. 22:36-40). Giving boldly affirms Christ's lordship. It is a blessed act that leads to joy.

Do you want to experience this kind of joy? I invite you to transfer your assets from earth to heaven. I invite you to give humbly, generously, and frequently to God's work. Excel in giving so that you can please God, serve others, and enjoy treasures in heaven. I urge you to embrace Christ's invitation:

GIVE, AND IT WILL BE GIVEN TO YOU. *LUKE 6:38*

Then when He gives you more, remind yourself why: so that you can give generously on every occasion.

I invite you to send your treasures on to heaven, where they will safely await you. When you do, you'll feel the freedom, experience the joy, and sense the smile of God.

Following is a six-step plan that will help keep you on the Treasure Principle track. It's a giving covenant between you and God. I encourage you to read it, discuss it with your spouse or friends, and pray about it.

My Giving Covenant

1. I affirm God's full ownership of me and everything entrusted to me. I recognize that my money and possessions are in fact His. I am His money manager. I will ask Him what He wants me to do with His money.
2. I will set aside the firstfruits—starting with at least 10 percent—of all I receive, treating it as holy and belonging exclusively to the Lord. I do this in obedience to Him, desiring His blessing. By faith I accept God's challenge to test Him in this matter.
3. From the remaining treasures God entrusts to me, I will seek to make generous freewill gifts. I recognize that God has entrusted wealth to me so that I can be generous on every occasion. Realizing that I can rob God by withholding not only the tithe but also the offerings He calls me to give, I ask Him to make His will clear to me.
4. I ask God to teach me to give sacrificially to His purposes, including helping the poor and reaching the lost. I commit myself to avoid indebtedness so that I don't tie up His funds and therefore feel greater freedom to follow the Spirit's promptings to give.
5. Recognizing that I cannot take earthly treasures from this world, I determine to collect them as heavenly treasures—for Christ's glory and the eternal good of others and myself. Affirming that heaven, not earth, is my home and that Christ is my Lord, I commit myself to lay out His assets before Him regularly, leaving nothing as untouchable, and ask His direction for what to do with His money and where to give it. I'll start with this question: What am I hanging on to that You want me to give away?
6. Recognizing that God has given me my family, my friends, my church, and others in my circle of influence, I ask Him to help me share the Treasure Principle with them so that they too can experience the greatest present joy and future reward.

If you sense that God is leading you to make these commitments to giving, sign below.

Signed ______________________________ Date _________

Write the six keys to the Treasure Principle.

1. ____
2. ____
3. ____
4. ____
5. ____
6. ____

THE DAY IN REVIEW

Review today's lesson.
What was the most important concept you read today?

____

How will this truth challenge you to be like Christ?

____

If you signed the covenant, ask God to help you take the steps to follow through. If you did not sign it, ask Him to help you grow in your willingness to recognize His ownership and to give to His kingdom. Write your prayer below.

____
____
____
____

[1]*The Barna Update* [online], 13 April 2004 [cited 5 January 2005]. Available from the Internet: *www.barna. org*. Used by permission.
[2]Charles Dickens, *A Christmas Carol,* in *Christmas Stories* (Cleveland: The World Publishing Company, 1946), 106.
[3]Ibid., 108–10.

Leader Guide

This leader guide provides suggestions for leading a small-group study of *The Treasure Principle.* Following this brief introduction, you will find step-by-step guidance for conducting each group session.

Learning Goals

After completing this study, members should be able to—

- state the Treasure Principle and six biblical keys to the Treasure Principle;
- affirm God's ownership of all things and their roles as God's money managers;
- list reasons collecting earthly treasures is unwise;
- state what it means to collect treasures in heaven;
- describe the way giving brings eternal rewards;
- commit to live by the Treasure Principle.

Resources

Order in advance one copy of *The Treasure Principle* (item 1-4158-2015-5) for each participant. To order, write to LifeWay Church Resources Customer Service; One LifeWay Plaza; Nashville, TN 37234-0113; fax (615) 251-5933; phone toll free (800) 458-2772; e-mail *orderentry@lifeway.com;* order online at *www.lifeway.com;* or visit a LifeWay Christian Store.

If couples are participating, stress that each person should have a copy of the workbook so that he or she can record individual responses to the learning activities.

Group Sessions

Plan for each session to last about an hour. Suggestions are provided to start discussion and to help participants review what they have studied during the week. More activities are provided than you will have time to use, so choose those that will best convey the key concepts in that week's material and will meet the needs of your group.

Study Options

Although this book contains four weeks of individual study, you and your group can choose between a four- and five-session group study.

Four-week plan. Omit the introductory session that follows and begin with session 1. If you choose this plan, you will need to give members their workbooks one week before the study begins so that they can complete their work in week 1 in advance of the first group session.

Five-week plan. The five-week plan begins with the following introductory session. If you choose this plan, you can wait until the introductory session to distribute workbooks because members do not need to prepare for this session.

Introductory Session

Learning Goals

After this session members will be able to—

- identify the goals of this course;
- identify the topics they will study in this course;
- summarize the study format of their workbooks.

Before the Session

1. Provide pens and name tags for participants. Place these on a table near the entrance to the meeting room. Make a name tag for yourself in advance.
2. Have workbooks available for distribution. Place them on the table with the name tags and pens.
3. Familiarize yourself with the content of the study by reading all four weeks.

During the Session

1. As participants arrive, introduce yourself and direct them to the name tags. Also have them pick up their workbooks.
2. After everyone has arrived, welcome the group. State that you look forward to the next four weeks of study, discussion, and fellowship.
3. Ask members to introduce themselves by stating their names and something they want to tell about themselves, such as how long they've lived in the community, where they were born, what their favorite sports team is, and so on. Use this time to help participants who might be uncomfortable speaking in front of others to feel more at ease. Limit this activity to 15 minutes.
4. Ask each member to give his or her expectations of this course. Ask, What motivated you to take this course?

5. State: During this study you will study Scripture to discover the way God views heavenly treasures and earthly treasures, and you'll make the important connection between your spiritual life and your finances. You'll realize the value of collecting heavenly treasures, and you'll learn how to make eternal investments by giving to God's kingdom. Present the learning goals for this course that are listed on page 94.
6. Ask members to open their workbooks to the contents page (p. 3) and have someone read the title of each week's study. Briefly preview each topic.
7. Have members turn to week 1 (p. 6). Explain that each week's material is divided into five days of study. Each day's study includes biblical content, commentary, and learning activities. Tell members to complete each week's study before the related group session. State that the study uses an interactive format. Encourage members to complete the learning activities as they study in order to delve into the Scriptures and to apply the material to their lives. Encourage members to complete one day's material at a time to get the most from their study. State that the weekly group sessions will provide opportunities for review and interaction.
8. Ask members to complete week 1 in their workbooks before the next group session. Instruct them to be ready to discuss the information they study in week 1 during next week's session. State that if they have questions while they are studying, they should write them in the margins of their books and ask them during the group session.
9. Close with a prayer praising God for His lordship over all our money and possessions. Ask Him to teach us the surpassing value of heavenly treasures and to give us a willingness to use our resources to serve Him.

Session 1
Investing in Eternity

Learning Goals

After this session members will be able to—

- acknowledge the connection between their money and their spiritual lives;
- identify biblical characters who were willing or unwilling to invest in eternity;
- list reasons collecting earthly treasures is unwise;
- state what it means to collect treasures in heaven;
- name three kinds of treasures that will last;
- describe ways God wants us to fulfill our desire for pleasure, possessions, and power;
- state the Treasure Principle.

Before the Session

1. Provide markers and name tags. Be sure to wear your name tag as people arrive.
2. Study and complete the activities in week 1.
3. Prepare three copies of an assignment slip with these questions: *What did the group ask John? How did John reply? How do you think the group felt when it heard his answer?*
4. Enlist four members to summarize the Scriptures in day 2 and to report on each character's willingness or unwillingness to invest in eternity: Zacchaeus, Luke 19:1-10; the early church, Acts 2:44-45; 4:32-35; the poor widow, Mark 12:41-44; the rich young man, Mark 10:17-22.
5. Make three placards: *Earthly treasures will be lost. Earthly treasures enslave. Earthly treasures tempt us to do evil.*
6. Make a placard with the Treasure Principle: *You can't take it with you, but you can send it on ahead.* Plan to display the placard at each session.

During the Session

1. Welcome everyone. Begin with prayer, asking God to bless your study and sharing together.
2. Tell the story of the Hebrew traveler in day 1. Ask: What did the traveler do when he found the treasure? Why? Read Matthew 13:44. Ask: To what did Jesus compare the treasure? What was Jesus saying about the kingdom? (It has immense value—worth giving up all you have to obtain.)
3. Ask a member to read Luke 3:1-15. Divide members into three groups. Ask one group to represent the crowds, another group to represent the tax collectors, and the other group to represent the soldiers. Distribute copies of the assignment slip you prepared and assign each group to answer the questions on the assignment slip. After time for group work, call for reports. Then ask the large group: What was John's point? (That the use of money held the key to each group's repenting and turning to God) What is the message for us? (Our money and our spiritual lives are connected.)
4. Call on the enlisted members to report on the willingness or unwillingness of Zacchaeus, the early church, the poor widow, and the rich young man to invest in eternity. After the final report, contrast the rich young man and the traveler introduced in day 1. Ask: What was each man willing to give to gain the kingdom? What did each man gain? State, The traveler made short-term sacrifices to obtain a long-term reward.
5. Ask a volunteer to read Matthew 6:19-21. Ask: Why did Jesus tell us not to collect treasures on earth? Where should we collect treasures? What is the meaning of verse 21?
6. Ask a volunteer to read Proverbs 23:4-5. Ask, Why is it unwise to collect earthly treasures? Allow members to respond; then display the placard that reads, *Earthly treasures will be lost.*
7. Ask a volunteer to read Matthew 6:24. Ask, Why is it unwise to collect earthly treasures? Allow members to respond; then display the placard that reads, *Earthly treasures enslave.*

8. Ask a volunteer to read 1 Timothy 6:9-10. Ask, Why is it unwise to collect earthly treasures? Allow members to respond; then display the placard that reads, *Earthly treasures tempt us to do evil.*
9. Read Matthew 6:20. Ask, What does it mean to collect treasures in heaven? (Investing in things that will last forever) Say, Treasure in heaven includes power, possessions, and pleasures. Acknowledge that Satan tempts us in each of these areas. Ask members to give their definitions of *hedonism, materialism,* and *egotism* on page 20. Explain how the desire for pleasure can degenerate into hedonism, the desire for possessions can turn into materialism, and the desire for power can become egotism. Ask members to identify ways Satan used these appeals in his temptation of Jesus in Luke 4:1-13 (p. 21).
10. Ask: Does this mean these desires are bad? (No, God built these desires into us; we must seek His ways of fulfilling them.) What are some ways God wants us to fulfill our desire for pleasure, possessions, and power? (Giving, prayer, fasting; p. 22) Challenge members to pursue pleasure, possessions, and power by investing in eternity.
11. Ask a volunteer to read Philippians 3:7-11. Ask: What is our ultimate treasure? (Christ) What are three kinds of treasure that will last? (Jesus, heaven, and eternal rewards; p. 24)
12. Quote John D. Rockefeller's accountant's statement on page 26. Display the placard with the Treasure Principle. Ask members to share the paraphrases they wrote on page 26. Challenge members to invest in what has lasting value.
13. Ask members to read the daily assignments and to complete the activities in week 2 before the next group session.
14. Close with a prayer asking God to help members understand the truth of the Treasure Principle and see their money and possessions from God's perspective.

Session 2

God Is the Owner

Learning Goals

After this session members will be able to—

- affirm God's ownership of all things;
- identify their responsibilities as God's money managers;
- identify three blessings that giving brings;
- describe the way giving brings eternal rewards;
- state the first and second keys to the Treasure Principle;
- identify ways they are making deposits on earth and in heaven.

Before the Session

1. Provide markers and name tags. Be sure to wear your name tag as people arrive.
2. Study and complete the activities in week 2.
3. Display the placard with the Treasure Principle.
4. Make placards with the first and second keys to the Treasure Principle:
   1. *God owns everything. I'm His money manager.*
   2. *My heart always goes where I put God's money.*
5. Enlist a member to study and explain the meaning of the parable in Luke 16:1-13.
6. Secure a recording of the song "Thank You (for Giving to the Lord)" by Ray Boltz.

During the Session

1. Welcome everyone. Begin with prayer, asking God to bless your study and sharing together.
2. Remind members of the author's experience with the court judgment. Ask: What was the result of this court judgment? How would you have responded? What did the author conclude about God? (God owns everything.)

3. Ask members to identify the things Job lost. Write these on a dry-erase board or chalkboard. Ask, How did Job respond to these disasters? Allow responses; then summarize by reading Job 1:20-22; 2:10. Ask, How was Job's attitude possible? (He recognized God's ownership.)
4. Ask for responses to the activity in the middle of page 32.
5. Ask four volunteers to read Deuteronomy 8:17-19; Psalm 24:1-2; Haggai 2:8; 1 Corinthians 6:19-20. After each passage is read, ask: Who is the owner? What does He own? Record responses on a dry-erase board or chalkboard.
6. Display the placard with the first key to the Treasure Principle: *God owns everything. I'm His money manager.* Ask: What's the difference between an owner and a manager (p. 34)? What are your responsibilities as God's money manager? List responses on a dry-erase board or chalkboard.
7. Ask a member to summarize Jesus' parable in Matthew 25:14-30. Introduce the concept of a manager's accountability (p. 36). Ask, What are some implications of our accountability as God's stewards? (We are required to be faithful with a little as well as with much. We are expected to give to God's kingdom purposes.) Challenge members to take time later to assess their faithfulness as God's money managers.
8. Divide members into three groups. Ask one group to read 2 Corinthians 8:1-5 and to identify the way giving brings joy, one group to read Isaiah 58:6-10 and to identify the way giving brings closeness to God, and the third group to read the last paragraph on page 40 and to identify the way giving brings freedom. Allow discussion; then call for reports.
9. State, Giving also brings eternal rewards. Have volunteers read Romans 2:6; Ephesians 6:8; Matthew 10:42. Ask, Why did Jesus instruct us to give to those who can't repay us? (So that He can give us spiritual rewards in heaven)
10. Explain that God keeps a record of our giving to His kingdom (see Mal. 3:16). State: By giving away God's property on earth, we will become property owners in heaven.

11. Call on the member enlisted to explain the meaning of the parable in Luke 16:1-13. Summarize by saying that God wants us to use His resources to make deposits in heaven.
12. Point to the placard with the Treasure Principle and ask members to recite it together.
13. Ask, What is your reaction to the concept of being motivated by rewards? Assure members that this is God's idea, not ours. Challenge them to think about the rewards their current giving habits are earning.
14. Play the song "Thank You (for Giving to the Lord)." Ask, How does this song depict our actions on earth?
15. Read Revelation 21:1-6. Say, We'll forever be with the person we were made for—Jesus—in a place made for us—heaven. Ask, Then why do many Christians dread the thought of leaving this world? (They don't want to leave the possessions they have collected on earth.)
16. Ask a volunteer to read Matthew 6:21. Show the placard with the second key to the Treasure Principle: *My heart always goes where I put God's money.* Ask, How does giving to missions give you a great heart for missions? Ask volunteers to share personal testimonies that support this key.
17. Ask members to complete the activity on page 48, if they haven't already done so, to identify ways they are making deposits on earth and in heaven. Say: Someone who spends his life moving away from his treasures has reason to despair. Someone who spends his life moving toward his treasures has reason to rejoice. Ask, Are you despairing or rejoicing?
18. Remove the placards from the walls and ask volunteers to repeat the Treasure Principle and the first two keys.
19. Ask members to read the daily assignments and to complete the activities in week 3 before the next group session.
20. Close with a prayer acknowledging God's ownership of all things. Ask Him to make us faithful managers.

Session 3
Heavenly Treasures

Learning Goals

After this session members will be able to—

- identify five roadblocks to giving;
- state the third, fourth, and fifth keys to the Treasure Principle;
- state what it means to live for the line;
- assess whether they are living for eternity;
- explain why money doesn't buy happiness and why things don't satisfy;
- identify why giving is the antidote to materialism.

Before the Session

1. Provide markers and name tags. Be sure to wear your name tag as people arrive.
2. Study and complete the activities in week 3.
3. Display the placard with the Treasure Principle.
4. Make placards with the third, fourth, and fifth keys to the Treasure Principle:

   3. Heaven, not earth, is my home.

   4. I should live not for the dot but for the line.

   5. Giving is the only antidote to materialism.
5. Prepare five slips of paper with one of the following road-blocks to giving on each slip: *unbelief, insecurity, pride, idolatry, the desire for power and control.*
6. Enlist a member to tell Jim Elliot's story (p. 56).

During the Session

1. Welcome everyone. Begin with prayer, asking God to bless your study and sharing together.
2. Divide members into five groups and give each group a slip of paper that identifies a roadblock to giving. Allow three minutes to brainstorm ways the assigned roadblocks could prevent someone from giving. Then call for reports.

3. Display the placard with the third key to the Treasure Principle: *Heaven, not earth, is my home.* Say, Mistaking earth for our home is the greatest deterrent to giving. Use 2 Corinthians 5:20; Hebrews 11:13,16 to emphasize that we are ambassadors for Christ, aliens on earth, and citizens of heaven. Ask for responses to the second activity on page 52 and to the first activity on page 53.
4. Point to the placard with the Treasure Principle and lead members to recite it together. Say, If we believe that heaven is our home, we should stop collecting treasures on earth and start sending more ahead to our true home.
5. Read the opening story in day 2. Emphasize that all of our possessions will eventually go to the junkyard.
6. Draw a dot and a line on a dry-erase board or chalkboard (p. 55). After explaining the concept, ask, What are some events on your dot?
7. Display the placard with the fourth key to the Treasure Principle: *I should live not for the dot but for the line.* Ask, What does it mean to live for the line? (Living for eternity, investing in heavenly treasures)
8. Call on the member enlisted to tell Jim Elliot's story. Ask, How did Jim Elliot live for the line?
9. Refer members to the second activity on page 57 ("If God audited …"). Challenge members to live for the line.
10. Ask, What is affluenza? (Materialism) Give examples (p. 58).
11. Read the statements by wealthy individuals on page 58. Ask for responses to the activity at the bottom of page 58 and to the activity on page 59. Ask, Why doesn't money buy happiness? Record responses on a dry-erase board or a chalkboard. State, We have one brief lifetime to use our resources to make a difference for eternity.
12. Refer to the activities on page 60 that call for members to write their obituaries based on their dots and again from heaven's perspective. Ask, What did you learn? Challenge members to make choices that reflect an eternal perspective.

13. Ask two volunteers to read Ecclesiastes 2:11; 5:10-15. Call for responses to the matching activity on page 63 (1. g, 2. d, 3. c, 4. e, 5. b, 6. h, 7. a, 8. f). Ask: What was Solomon's conclusion? Why don't things satisfy? Record responses on a dry-erase board or a chalkboard. Ask, Why do we keep getting fooled into thinking that things will satisfy? (Because our hearts yearn for treasure, we mistake earthly treasures for eternal ones.)
14. Summarize Jesus' parable in Luke 12:13-21. Ask: Was this man living for the dot or the line? What does it mean to be rich toward God? (Collecting treasures in heaven)
15. Ask, If affluenza is the disease, what's the cure? Ask a volunteer to read 1 Timothy 6:17-19. Ask, How did Paul instruct us to be rich? (Good works, generosity, collecting treasures in heaven) Show the placard with the fifth key to the Treasure Principle: *Giving is the only antidote to materialism.* Ask, How does giving combat materialism? (Reminds us that God is the owner and we are His servants, helps us focus on heavenly rather than earthly treasures)
16. Read C. S. Lewis's statement on page 68. Ask, What do you think that means? (Too often we settle for a life spent acquiring materials possessions instead of eternal treasures.)
17. Use the activity at the bottom of page 68 to remind members of things they can give besides money.
18. Ask members to brainstorm creative ways they can give. Record these on a dry-erase board or chalkboard.
19. Ask members to read the daily assignments and to complete the activities in week 4 before the next group session.
20. Review keys 3–5 by drawing attention to the placards and leading members to read them together.
21. Close by confessing to God that materialism doesn't make us happy. Pray that God will help members make hard decisions and set new priorities that will allow them to live for the line and invest in heavenly treasures.

Session 4
Collecting Treasures

Learning Goals

After this session members will be able to—

- define *tithe* and state its importance;
- identify reasons to give now;
- explain why God distributes wealth unevenly;
- identify ways believers can distribute wealth;
- state the sixth key to the Treasure Principle;
- identify ways to collect treasures in heaven;
- sign a giving covenant to indicate commitments they are willing to make.

Before the Session

1. Provide markers and name tags. Be sure to wear your name tag as people arrive.
2. Study and complete the activities in week 4.
3. Display the placard with the Treasure Principle.
4. Enlist three members to use the material on pages 80–81 in day 3 to summarize the three reasons to give now. Ask the members to use the suggested Scriptures in day 3.
5. Have available a slip of paper and a pen or pencil for each member.
6. Make a placard with the sixth key to the Treasure Principle:

   6. God prospers me not to raise my standard of living but to raise my standard of giving.
7. Make a poster that lists all six keys to the Treasure Principle; however, use blanks in the place of several important words. Be prepared to display the poster at the appropriate time.

During the Session

1. Welcome everyone. Begin with prayer, asking God to bless your study and sharing together.

2. Ask a volunteer to define *tithe.* (Tenth) Read Leviticus 27:30; Proverbs 3:9; Malachi 3:8-10. State that God commands that we give Him the first tenth of our income.
3. Ask a volunteer to read Matthew 23:23. Ask: What were the scribes and Pharisees willing to give? What did they neglect? In what way does Jesus' response validate the tithe?
4. Present the statistics about giving on page 73. Ask: Do Christians give more or less than the tithe? (Less) Why do Christians give so little to God?
5. Ask members to state reasons tithing is important for believers (p. 74). List these on a dry-erase board or chalkboard. Point to the placard with the Treasure Principle. Ask, How does tithing help you collect treasures in heaven?
6. Explain the meaning of *freewill offerings* (p. 75). Read 2 Corinthians 9:7. Use 2 Corinthians 9:13 to explain that God also expects our obedience in giving freewill offerings.
7. Ask a volunteer to read Deuteronomy 16:10,16-17. Ask, How are we to give? (In proportion to God's blessing, suited to our means, according to God's blessing)
8. Read again Malachi 3:10. Ask members to identify the blessings God promises when we tithe. Say: many people can't afford to give precisely because they are not giving. God promised to bless us when we give.
9. Recount the story about Scott Lewis and Bill Bright on pages 78–79. Challenge members to start with the tithe and move beyond the tithe by giving freewill offerings.
10. Call on the three members enlisted to summarize from day 3 the three reasons to give now. Distribute slips of paper and pens or pencils. Ask members to write down the three reasons as they are discussed. After the reports, review by asking members to identify the three reasons.
11. Present the author's argument against leaving a large inheritance to children. Read 1 Peter 1:3-4 and emphasize that the most important inheritance is imperishable, uncorrupted, and unfading.

12. Read Luke 6:38. Ask, Was Jesus teaching a prosperity gospel? (No, God's blessing may or may not be material wealth.)
13. Read 2 Corinthians 9:10-11. Ask, Why does God give wealth to many people? (So that we can give generously) Display the placard with the sixth key to the Treasure Principle: *God prospers me not to raise my standard of living but to raise my standard of giving.* Emphasize the responsibilities of managing the wealth God has given (p. 86).
14. Read Proverbs 30:8-9. Discuss the true/false statements on page 87. Summarize that God distributes wealth unevenly so that His children can give it to one another on His behalf. Ask, How can believers distribute their wealth? List responses on a dry-erase board or chalkboard.
15. Tell the end of the story about the court judgment against the author (p. 88). Ask: Why did the author refuse the royalty payments? How was he blessed by this decision? (The joy of giving more to God's kingdom)
16. Point to the placard with the Treasure Principle and lead members to recite it. Ask members to identify the ways to collect treasures in heaven that they studied this week. (Tithing, freewill offerings, giving now, distributing wealth) List these on a dry-erase board or chalkboard.
17. Display the poster listing the incomplete keys to the Treasure Principle. Ask volunteers to state the keys, filling in the blanks with the correct words. Assist as needed. Issue a challenge to live by the six keys.
18. Have volunteers read aloud the six points in the giving covenant on page 92. Challenge members to discover the freedom and joy that come from giving and to sign the covenant on page 93 if they have not already done so.
19. Ask members to pray in pairs that they will follow through on their commitments. Close by praying that God will help members collect treasures in heaven as they share what God has given to them.

In the **Christian Growth Study Plan** *The Treasure Principle* is a resource for course credit in the subject area Personal Life in the Christian Growth category of plans. To receive credit, read the book; complete the learning activities; show your work to your pastor, a staff member, or a church leader; then complete the following information. This page may be duplicated. Send the completed page to:

Christian Growth Study Plan
One LifeWay Plaza; Nashville, TN 37234-0117
Fax (615) 251-5067; e-mail ***cgspnet@lifeway.com***

For information about the Christian Growth Study Plan, refer to the *Christian Growth Study Plan Catalog*, located online at *www.lifeway.com/cgsp*. If you do not have access to the Internet, contact the Christian Growth Study Plan office, (800) 968-5519, for the specific plan you need for your ministry.

The Treasure Principle
COURSE NUMBER: CG-1067

PARTICIPANT INFORMATION

Social Security Number (USA ONLY-optional)	Personal CGSP Number*	Date of Birth (MONTH, DAY, YEAR)
- -	- -	- -

Name (First, Middle, Last)	Home Phone
	- -

Address (Street, Route, or P.O. Box)	City, State, or Province	Zip/Postal Code

Email Address for CGSP use

Please check appropriate box: ❑ Resource purchased by church ❑ Resource purchased by self ❑ Other

CHURCH INFORMATION

Church Name

Address (Street, Route, or P.O. Box)	City, State, or Province	Zip/Postal Code

CHANGE REQUEST ONLY

☐ Former Name		
☐ Former Address	City, State, or Province	Zip/Postal Code
☐ Former Church	City, State, or Province	Zip/Postal Code

Signature of Pastor, Conference Leader, or Other Church Leader	Date

*New participants are requested but not required to give SS# and date of birth. Existing participants, please give CGSP# when using SS# for the first time. Thereafter, only one ID# is required. **Mail to:** Christian Growth Study Plan, One LifeWay Plaza, Nashville, TN 37234-0117. Fax: (615)251-5067.

Revised 4-05